Pottery

Pottery

David Winkley

DRAKE PUBLISHERS INC

New York

Published in 1974 by
Drake Publishers Inc.
381 Park Avenue South
New York, New York 10016

© 1974 by David Winkley

Library of Congress Cataloging in Publication Data

Winkley, David.
Pottery.

1.   Pottery.   I.   Title.
NK4225.W53   738.3   74-4058

ISBN 0-87749-661-7

Printed in the United States of America.

Contents

Illustrations

Acknowledgements

I would like to thank Andrew Priddy for his patient help in taking all the black and white and many of the colour photographs in this book; Geoffrey Doonan, John Harlow, Colin Kellam, and Jane and Ian Read for advice and help with some of the methods of hand-building, and for supplying photographs of their work; the Bristol City Museum and Art Gallery for permission to reproduce colour plates 1 and 4; the Trustees of the British Museum for permission to reproduce colour plates 2, 3 and 5; Mrs. Sheila Sharp and Mrs. E. Harvey for typing the manuscript.

Above all I would thank Bernard Forrester who introduced me to the pleasures of making pots by hand for all his kind and generous help and encouragement.

D.W.

Pottery

Introduction

The pleasure and satisfaction of making pots by hand is something deep and immediate. It springs from working simply and directly with the most responsive of all natural materials – clay. Nothing could be more humble yet offer such rich opportunities for creative and imaginative work. But it is also the transformation of clay by fire that makes pottery such a unique and fascinating craft. Fire makes clay hard and permanent, but it also does more: it introduces an element of chance into the business of making so that the experience of taking your still-warm pots from the kiln remains always fresh and exciting.

This book describes all the ways in which pots can be made by hand. It covers the various techniques of preparing, forming and decorating clay; how to mix and apply slips and glazes; and how to design, build and fire small kilns. I hope that beginners will find it a sound basis for creative claywork, and also that it will stimulate those with some experience to explore aspects of pottery making in more depth.

No attempt has been made to encourage more convenient methods at the expense of what ought to be the real reasons for making anything by hand. I feel strongly that the intrinsic qualities of warmth and vitality which characterise all good hand-made pots and which distinguish them from their machine-made counterparts are more likely to grow from the use of natural earthy materials fired in a living flame than from the sole use of prepared clays and glazes fired in electric kilns. It is rather like using some convenience foods: they may be quick and easy, but too often something of the essential flavour is lost by the way.

Throughout this book I have also stressed the importance of technical knowledge and the sound choice of materials and equipment – solely because if they are ignored or neglected much valuable creative work may be lost. From a sound knowledge of the possibilities and limitations of clay and of the basic processes of making, your confidence and skill will surely grow. And with them your satisfaction and enjoyment.

Those last two things are what making pots by hand is really all about.

A Glossary of Potters' Terms

ALUMINA: One of the two principal ingredients of feldspar and hence of all clays. It is very refractory melting at 2040°C (3704°F).

ASH: Wood and vegetable ashes are used as a fluxing ingredient in some stoneware glazes.

ATOMISING: The breaking down of oil into very tiny particles by means of air pressure so that it burns more readily.

BAG WALL: A wall built inside the kiln to protect the pots from direct flame impingement.

BAITING: The single stoking of a kiln with wood.

BALL CLAY: Plastic secondary clay so called because of the former practice in England of transporting the clay in the shape of large balls.

BATT: A word used by potters to describe almost any flat surface on which to work or fire clay, e.g. drying slabs, throwing discs, kiln shelves.

BISCUIT: A preliminary firing before glazing which transforms the clay into pottery; unglazed fired pottery.

BODY: The clay or mixture of clays and other materials of which pots are made.

BUNG: A stack of saggers or shelves of pots in a kiln.

CELADON: A French term for green or green-grey stoneware and porcelain glazes.

CHARGING: Packing pots in the kiln for firing.

CHATTER: Uneven marks on leather-hard pots caused by the vibration of a turning tool.

CHEMICALLY COMBINED WATER:	Water which became part of the molecular structure of clay during its formation by weathering. It is driven off between 400°C and 500°C (752°F and 932°F) and once it is lost the clay becomes pottery.
CHINA CLAY:	White primary clay derived from decomposed feldspathic rock; kaolin.
CLAM:	To seal the kiln with a clay/sand mixture.
COILING:	A method of building pots using ropes or coils of clay.
COLLARING:	Reducing the diameter of a spinning pot by outside pressure of both hands.
COLLOIDAL:	Sticky or gluey.
CONES:	Small pyramids of glaze materials which bend and melt to indicate the degree of heat attained in the kiln.
CRACKLE:	Intentional decorative fissures which form in a glaze. They are caused by the glaze shrinking more than the clay on cooling.
CRAZING:	As crackle, only unintentional.
CRYSTALLISATION:	The formation of crystals in some slowly cooling glazes.
DAMPER:	A sliding cast-iron or clay plate inserted in a flue or chimney and used to control the draught through the kiln.
DECANT:	To pour off surplus water from the top of a settled glaze or slip.
DIPPING:	Immersing pots in a slip or glaze.
DOWN-DRAUGHT KILN:	One in which the heat passes down through the pots and exits at the same level as it entered the kiln.
DRAWING A KILN:	Removing fired pots from the kiln.
DRAW TRIAL:	A small ring of glazed clay hooked out of the kiln to gauge the progress of a firing.

DUNTING: Cracking of pots caused by strains during cooling or by cold draughts of air striking the pots as they cool.

EARTHENWARE: Any kind of fired pottery with a porous body whether glazed or not.

ENGOBE: Slip; liquid clay.

FAIENCE: A term loosely applied to all glazed earthenware. Originally it referred to decorated tin-glazed earthenware made at Faenza in Italy.

FAT CLAY: Highly plastic clay.

FELDSPAR: A white crystal found in granite comprising silica, alumina and a flux in the form of sodium, potassium or calcium. Feldspar is the matrix of clay.

FIREBOX: The part of a kiln where combustion of the fuel takes place.

FIRECLAY: Highly refractory clay found usually between coal seams.

FIRING: The heating of pots in a kiln.

FLATWARE: Plates, saucers, dishes, bowls etc.; pots with their widest extremity at the rim.

FLUES: Spaces through which flames and gases pass in and out of the kiln.

FLUX: A substance which promotes or helps others to melt.

FORMA: A support.

FRIT: A glaze ingredient made of a glass which has been heated, rapidly cooled and then ground to a powder.

FUSIBLE CLAYS: Those clays which vitrify and lose their shape below 1200°C (2192°F).

GLASSIFY: To melt to a glass.

GLOST FIRING: Glaze firing.

GREENWARE: Unfired pottery.

GROG: Non-plastic material added to plastic clays to reduce shrinkage and warping. It can take the form of powdered and graded fired clay, sand or flint.

HARP: A U-shaped metal or wooden tool, across the ends of which a wire is held taut. Used for cutting clay.

KAOLIN: See China Clay.

OXYDISED FIRING: One in which sufficient air is always present to ensure complete combustion of the fuel.

PLACING: Packing pots in the kiln for firing.

PLASTER OF PARIS: The common term for gypsum or calcium sulphate. It is used to make clay drying slabs and for dish moulds.

PLASTICITY: That characteristic of ball clays which enables them to be freely manipulated and to hold the shapes imposed on them.

PORCELAIN: A refinement of stoneware made from china clay, feldspar and quartz. It is high fired, white, vitrified and translucent when thin.

PRIMARY CLAYS: China clays; those found on the site of the parent rock from which they were formed.

PUGMILL: A machine for mixing and compressing plastic clays. It consists of a cylinder containing revolving helical blades which chop, mix and homogenise the clay.

PYROMETER: An instrument for measuring the temperature inside a kiln.

RAW GLAZE: Either a glaze containing a high proportion of plastic clay applied to greenware; or a glaze containing no fritted material.

REDUCTION FIRING: A firing with incomplete combustion of the fuel during the melting of the glazes. Carbon robs metallic oxides of their oxygen and reduces them to their metallic state.

REFRACTORY CLAYS: The opposite of fusible: those clays which are highly resistant to heat, e.g. china clays and fireclays.

SAGGER: A refractory fireclay box to contain pots and protect them from direct flame impingement during firing. Probably a corruption of the word 'safeguard'.

SALT GLAZE: A method of glazing by throwing salt (sodium chloride) into the kiln. At stoneware temperatures it volatilises and the soda combines with silica in the clay to form a glaze.

SETTING CHAMBER: That part of the kiln where pots are placed for firing.

SGRAFFITO: The decoration of leather-hard pots by scratching through a layer of slip to reveal the contrasting colour of the clay below.

SHARDS: Pieces of broken pottery.

SHORT CLAY: Non-plastic clay or clay with poor working properties.

SINTER POINT: The temperature at which glaze ingredients begin to melt.

SKEWBACK: A wedge-shaped brick from which the kiln arch springs.

SLAKE: To moisten dry clay with water.

SLIP: Liquid clay; engobe.

SLIP GLAZE: A glaze made mostly from clay and applied to green-ware.

SLIPWARE: Earthenware decorated by contrasting layers and trailings of slip under a lead glaze.

SLURRY: A stiff mixture of clay and water.

SOAK: To hold the kiln steady at its maximum temperature.

SOURING: The storing and ageing of clay to increase plasticity.

SPURS: Refractory triangular supports which prevent earthenware glazed on the underside from sticking to the kiln shelf.

STACK: To set pots in the kiln.

15

STONEWARE: A tough impermeable pottery fired between 1250°C and 1350°C (2280°F and 2462°F) at which temperature the clay body vitrifies.

TENMOKU: A rich black stoneware glaze containing a high proportion of iron oxide. It often runs to a rust red where thin on rims and handles etc.

THROWING: The shaping of pottery forms from plastic clay on a potter's wheel.

TIN-GLAZE WARES: Earthenware covered by a glaze made white and opaque by the addition of tin oxide to the glaze mix.

TOOTH: Roughness or coarse grain in a clay.

TURNING: The shaving and trimming of leather-hard clay from the walls or base of pots. It is done on the potter's wheel with a metal shaving tool.

VISCOSITY: The relative thickness or stickiness of a liquid.

VITRIFY: To fire to the point of glassification so that the clay becomes hard and impermeable.

WEATHERING: The breaking down of rocks by action of the elements rain, wind, ice etc.

WEDGING: The repeated cutting and beating of plastic clay to remove all air and to render the whole mass homogenous.

Chapter 1

Clay

THE ORIGINS OF CLAY

Within the brief span of our own lifetime the rocks which form the hard crust of the earth appear unchanging and everlasting. But on a larger time scale measured in hundreds of millions of years the underlying structure of the landscape has undergone profound changes. Nature is continuously and relentlessly battering and eroding the whole surface of the earth, breaking down rocks into smaller and smaller particles.

All the elements of Nature play a part in this weathering process, but that played by water is the most significant. Its power to break down seemingly impervious rock is incalculable. Over millions of years water must literally have washed away mountains.

The weathering of granite is of special importance to potters. An igneous rock, one that has been spewed up in a molten state from the depths of the earth, granite contains crystals of feldspar and it is the decomposition of this particular material which results in the formation of clays. Feldspar is composed mainly of silica and alumina, and it is so common and widespread that it makes up nearly 60% of the earth's crust. Clay, in consequence, is abundantly found in almost every part of the world.

Clays also occur in great variety. Some are pure white in colour, others tan, grey, buff or red (terra cotta). They also vary greatly in the amount of heat they will withstand in the kiln. Some clays will deform and even melt at comparatively low temperatures (fusible clays), while others are capable of withstanding extremes of heat (refractory clays). But whatever their apparent characteristics, clays are divided into only two main categories – *primary* or *secondary* clays – according to the way in which they were formed geologically. As we shall see this greatly determines their particular usefulness for the craft potter.

Primary clays are the rarer of the two kinds and are more commonly known as china clays or kaolins. They are found on the same site as the rocks from which they were formed – and they were mainly formed, it is now thought, by chemical action from below rather than by weathering from above.

China clays have had little opportunity to become contaminated by other materials, and as a result they are very pure, and usually white or creamy in colour. Their purity gives them a high degree of refractoriness but, because of their comparatively large particle size, they lack the plasticity associated with less pure clays. China clays are extensively used in the production of industrial whitewares and in the manufacture of high-temperature bricks, crucibles and insulators. They also find their way into paints, paper and plastics.

For the hand potter china clay is the basis of plastic porcelain bodies. It is also used to modify other clays, and is an invaluable ingredient in both high- and low-temperature glazes.

Secondary clays, often called ball clays, are common and abundant. They differ from china clay in that they are transported by water away from their rocky matrices and laid down in beds on plains or in river estuaries, wherever water flows more gently. In the move from one site to another they become intermixed with organic, vegetable and carbonaceous matter and with other minerals, especially iron. The presence of these additional materials gives ball clays a wide range of colour in the raw state. Most of it disappears on firing, leaving the clay a buff or light grey colour.

For potters, most ball clays possess above all one important and fascinating characteristic – plasticity. Unlike china clays they can be very readily shaped and, provided that they have been suitably treated, they will hold the forms imposed on them through the subsequent processes of drying and firing.

Among natural materials plasticity is unique to clay. It arises partly from the shape and size of the clay particles themselves and partly from geological and bacterial action. In their journey away from the site of the parent rock the action of water grinds the clay particles particularly small and they assume a flat, plate-like shape, so that each particle has virtually only two dimensions, length and breadth. This structure is very different from that of non-plastic materials, which is always in three dimensions forming a lattice. The presence of water and organic matter in the clay helps to form colloidal or sticky gels around each flat particle, binding them together while at the same time allowing them to slide against one another.

The varied colours and textures of ball clays, together with their high degree of plasticity, make them particularly suitable for making pots by hand. It is with these plastic clays that we shall mostly concern ourselves throughout this book.

THE DIFFERENT KINDS OF POTTERY
Potters classify their wares by the temperatures at which they are fired. In ascending order of heat these are earthenware, stoneware and porcelain. Some pottery is tougher and, therefore, more durable than others, some brighter in colour, but from a creative point of view no one kind is any better than another. There have been outstanding ceramic achievements at all temperature ranges and infinite possibilities for personal expression exist, whichever one you choose to work in.

Earthenware is the oldest kind of pottery and the most common: pottery of the past and present was and is very largely of this kind. It is fired between

700°C (1292°F) and 1150°C (2102°F), at which temperatures the clay is reasonably hard – especially in the higher part of the temperature range – but still porous. A glaze is needed to make it watertight and hygenic in use. Earthenware includes the following kinds of pottery:

RAKU. A term loosely applied to very low-fired, soft-glazed ware made from coarse open clay which enables it to withstand rapid changes of temperature during firing. It takes its name from a specific kind of Japanese pottery often used for tea ceremonies.

TERRA COTTA. This roughly describes almost all porous, unglazed pottery. It is usually, but not invariably, made from red clay, although it can be pale brown, buff or black. Almost all primitive pottery and much garden pottery, such as plant pots – now sadly being replaced by plastic – is of this kind.

SLIPWARE. A name given to pots made usually from red clay and decorated by layers or trailings of contrasting liquid clay (slip). It was traditionally covered by a soft transparent glaze with an amber tinge made from lead sulphide (galena).

MAJOLICA. An Italian term for high-fired earthenware made from pale clay covered with a glaze made white and opaque by the addition of tin oxide (tin-glaze ware). It is decorated in bright colours, usually blue, green, pink and yellow. Depending on where it was made, it is also called Delft or Faience.

FINE EARTHENWARE. This is high-fired earthenware made from pale or buff clay, usually decorated and covered with glazes of various colours and textures.

The classifications are not rigid and some techniques particular to one kind are often combined with those used for another.

Stoneware is denser, tougher and more durable than earthenware. It is fired between 1250°C (2282°F) and 1350°C (2462°F). At these higher temperatures stoneware clays vitrify: that is, the particles of clay fuse together and the ware becomes impervious to liquids.

Stoneware has particular tactile appeal – it really makes you want to touch and hold it. The textures of both clay and glaze are often lovely in themselves, and very attractive stoneware can be made without any additional decoration. It has nothing like the colour range of earthenware because few colouring agents survive at high temperatures, but any lack of brightness is amply compensated by the subtlety of stoneware colours.

Apart from ordinary glazed ware the only other kind of stoneware is salt-glazed. Common salt, sodium chloride, is thrown into the kiln at the height of the firing whereupon it volatilizes. The extreme heat causes the sodium in the salt to combine with silica in the clay to form a thin glaze with a surface texture rather like that of an orange-skin. Many splendid bottles called *bellarmines* and decorated with impressed clay seals were salt-glazed in Germany during the fifteenth and sixteenth centuries, but today salt-glazing is confined almost exclusively to the manufacture of vitrified drainage pipes.

Porcelain is a refinement of stoneware. It is based on china clay, and when fired between 1300°C (2372°F) and 1450°C (2642°F) is extremely tough, white and vitreous, and translucent if thin. When struck it has a clear bell-like ring, and at its best a clear flawless glaze surface.

Porcelain should not be confused with *bone-china*, the translucency of which is induced by adding calcined animal bones to the clay body. It is fired at a lower temperature and has neither the hardness of glaze nor toughness of body of true porcelain.

CHOOSING YOUR CLAY

Different kinds of pottery require different kinds of clay. When fired, each kind – whether it is porous or vitrified – should be just hard and tough enough to serve the purpose for which it was made. You can, of course, slightly modify a clay yourself by adding a small amount of another kind to it. The temperature at which a clay matures (that is, becomes hard and tough without distorting) can be lowered by the addition of a more fusible clay, or raised by adding a more refractory one, such as fireclay or china clay.

But only so much can be done in this way. As there are so many different kinds of clay available a better course is to consult clay manufacturers or potters' suppliers as to the suitability of the various clays they offer for the particular kinds of ware you want to make.

Obtaining clays should be an easy matter wherever you live. Clay manu-facturers offer by far the widest range, usually packed in powder form. Potters' suppliers sell it both powdered and ready prepared, though the choice is more limited and the cost a little higher. Keep in mind that clay is heavy, bulky stuff, and that freight charges will be high if you live a long way from the source of supply. It will be more economical to buy in larger quantities, and it is well worth while joining with others to purchase raw materials in bulk if you can.

There may be a source of supply much nearer home. A nearby brick, tile or drainage pipe works will often sell prepared coarse clays ideal for some kinds of pottery making like hand-building. A local workshop potter is also worth approaching: I often supply clay to teachers or neighbours who are hobby potters. Most interesting, too, because clay is so widespread you can dig and prepare your own, although this can be hard work!

Two kinds of prepared plastic clay, one red terra cotta and the other grey or buff stoneware, are probably best to begin with. With them, you can get on sooner with the more exciting job of actually making pots. But don't preclude experimenting with other kinds of clay once you have gained some experience.

CLAY PREPARATION

Prepared plastic clay delivered from a potters' supplier will have been already mixed in a special machine, rather like a large mincer, called a pug-mill. It should require little further preparation beyond wedging and kneading described below. With some very well prepared clays you can dispense with wedging and just knead them.

Powdered clay needs more preparation. It's a rather dusty operation, so wear some kind of protective face mask and mix it out of doors if you can. Put the clay in a large polythene (polyethelene) bowl or tub. If you are blending two or more clays together, or adding sand or grog (a non-plastic material added to reduce shrinkage and warping), put a proportion of each into the tub consecutively. Adding all of first one and then the other will make it more difficult to mix them evenly.

Add sufficient clean water to make a very sloppy mixture or slip, stirring to ensure that all the clay is thoroughly wet. The best tools for stirring are your hand and arm. When mixed, pour the slip into plaster-of-Paris troughs or onto slabs of biscuit-fired clay and leave to stiffen. (Drying slabs are easily made by pouring a 2 in. thickness of plaster into cardboard cartons and allowing it to set.)

Dry larger quantities of clay by joining together several drying slabs. Raise them off the ground so that air can circulate freely and build a low wall of bricks around the edges of the slabs to contain the clay. A dry crust may form at the edges from time to time and this should be pushed back into the middle of the slip where it will gradually soften again. Eventually the whole mass will stiffen to a reasonably homogenous consistency.

In dry climates it is a simple matter to dig a pit in the ground say six feet by four and six to nine inches deep. Line this with calico or hessian to keep the clay clean, pour in the slurry and cover with a piece of similar material. The water content of the clay will gradually seep into the ground through the bottom sheet while the top one acts as a wick drawing the moisture upwards and speeding evaporation. If there is occasional rain the clay can be covered temporarily.

Remove the clay from the slabs or pit as soon as it has dried to a workable consistency. Only experience will enable you to judge this, but as a general guide the clay should be soft but not sticky. Wedge it briefly before storing it.

Avoid the temptation to make too stiff a mixture initially in the mistaken belief that it will save time. Maximum plasticity depends on every clay particle being thoroughly wet, and newly prepared stiff clay will ultimately take longer than slip to reach a good plastic workable condition.

Digging your own clay. Despite the extra labour involved, making pots from clay which you have dug and prepared yourself is particularly satisfying. Children and students respond very readily to the opportunity for simple experiment and research that the use of locally found raw materials provides. The chances are that any clay in your neighbourhood will be fusible and therefore suitable only for earthenware.

Remembering that most clay is transported by water, a good place to begin prospecting is on river banks or by river estuaries. It may emerge as a shiny mass in either place, or it may be a foot or two below the level of the soil. Those who work or dig the land – farmers, builders, construction workers – will often be able to tell you where clay can be found.

After digging dry the clay thoroughly. Then break it into small pieces and soak it until it becomes a thick slip. Drying the clay first helps to facilitate the formation of this: clay which contains some moisture strongly resists further softening.

Pass the slip first through a garden sieve to remove stones, wood or foreign matter and then through an 80- or 100-mesh sieve to remove coarse particles. If you intend adding any non-plastic material such as sand or grog do it after the second sieving, and then dry as for powdered clay above.

Before making in any quantity with locally dug clay test it first with one or two small pots. To be workable some local clays may need to be mixed with others from suppliers. Some may prove unsatisfactory for making pots but they may be valuable as a glaze ingredient. I gather a clay of this kind from a nearby beach.

Reclaiming clay. Besides its other unique properties clay which has been used can also be reclaimed, provided that it has not been fired.

Sloppy clay from wheel trays should be dried like new clay on slabs or in troughs, and clay which is only a little too soft can be quickly stiffened by rolling it into coils and then bending them into hoops on a board. Clay which is only a little too stiff may be cut into layers and softer clay spread between them prior to wedging.

Very hard clay should be dried thoroughly, slaked down in water and then dried again to a workable consistency.

Take especial care when removing clay from plaster slabs. Always pull the clay off with your hands and not with the aid of a metal scraper. Plaster is hygroscopic and even a tiny piece will spoil a pot by reabsorbing moisture from the atmosphere, causing the clay or glaze above it to crack and flake off. In severe cases a pot may burst because of plaster in the body. It is safer to discard ruthlessly any clay contaminated by plaster.

Storing clay. All clay, whether new or reclaimed, will improve with keeping. The 'shortness' or lack of plasticity of newly prepared clay is especially marked. After a month or so plasticity is noticably improved due to the formation of colloidal gels and to thorough soaking of the clay particles. The ancient oriental potters used to store clay for their children in much the same way that some parents lay down fine wines for theirs.

The addition of older mature clay to a newly made batch helps to speed the increase of plasticity. You can test that clay has reached a good working condition by winding a small coil of it round your finger. When it is mature it should bend easily without cracking.

If air is excluded prepared clay will remain soft and workable for several months, even years if kept cool and damp. Polythene or P.V.C. bags and sheeting, provided they have no holes in them, are ideal for keeping small quantities. Larger amounts keep well in galvanised or polythene tubs. I keep very large quantities of clay ageing for up to a year in old galvanised metal corn bins and coal bunkers. If the container is not completely full place a polythene sheet over the clay before putting on the lid.

PREPARING CLAY FOR WORKING

To make successful pots by any method you must have well-prepared clay. It should be of even consistency and free from air pockets. Industrially this is done in de-airing pugmills which extract air from the clay by passing it through a vacuum. Hand potters achieve a similar condition by *wedging* and *kneading*.

You will need a firm, stout table or bench with a good clean surface on which you can bang the clay really hard. An old kitchen table, providing it is robust, will serve the purpose, or you can easily construct one yourself from bricks or building blocks using a reinforced paving slab for the top (fig. 1). I use an old table topped with marble, which is a lovely smooth and slightly absorbant surface on which to prepare clay. Plastic laminate tops are unsuitable because clay sticks to them very readily.

For most efficient and comfortable working the wedging bench should not be too high. With your arm resting by your side the tips of your fingers should just touch the top.

1 A simple wedging bench built from building blocks and a reinforced paving slab.

You will also need a wire to cut the clay. Fine twisted stainless steel is best, but thick nylon fishing line is also satisfactory. For a good grip fix handles at each end. Anything to hand can be used for these – pieces of grooved dowel, coat toggles, brass curtain rings or large washers.

A paint scraper is also handy for keeping the bench clean.

Wedging   removes any air pockets and brings the clay to an even consistency. It will, incidentally, also give you a good idea as to the state of the clay: wedging is impossible with clay which is too soft and sticky.

Take a lump weighing between 20 and 30 lb. and knock it roughly into a cube. Arrange it on the wedging bench so that half projects over the edge facing you. Take the wire taut between both hands and, cutting swiftly upwards, slice off the overhanging piece. Put your knee under it to prevent it falling. Take the cut piece, raise it at arm's length above your head and bang it down hard onto the piece remaining on the bench. After each banging down tap the edges of the clay to prevent protruding pieces from trapping air in the mass. Then knock the whole roughly into a cube again, give it half a turn and repeat the process. Make sure that each successive cut with the wire is at right angles to the previous one.

The number of times you will need to do this depends very much on the state of the clay initially. If it is new, prepared clay from the suppliers or from drying slabs it should be in fairly good condition already and 15 or 20 times will be sufficient. Reclaimed clay of very uneven consistency, however, will need wedging until you can feel no hard lumps when cutting with the wire and the cross-section of clay appears smooth and homogenous.

Very small amounts of clay may be wedged simply by tearing the lump in half and banging it from hand to hand.

Kneading   finally prepares the clay for working. It removes any remaining air pockets and improves plasticity by aligning the clay particles more closely. There are two methods you can use. The first is easier, but the second more effectively prepares clay for throwing. With both methods the clay is moved from the edge of the mass into the centre and out to the edge again.

OX-HEAD KNEADING   is a method which uses both hands to press the clay. After wedging cut the lump of clay in half. Take one of the pieces weighing between 10 and 15 lb. and rock it backwards and forwards on the bench to form a cylinder about 10 inches long. With your hands at either end of this, push the clay away from you while simultaneously pressing inwards and downwards with the fleshy part of both hands. After half a dozen rhythmic movements like this a shape similar to an ox head will develop. Prevent the 'horns' from getting too long by putting your fingers behind them and pulling them in towards the centre of the mass. After each downward and inward movement with both hands, skip your fingers around the shape prior to pulling it back onto its 'nose'. This will ensure that the pressure of each successive downward movement is on a different part of the clay. If done correctly you should see a spiral develop on either side of the 'nose' as the clay folds over onto itself (fig. 2). After several minutes of this kneading the clay will be ready for use.

ORIENTAL SPIRAL KNEADING uses the right hand only to press the clay; the left merely steadies the mass and creates a spiral movement by gradually turning the clay in a circle.

Begin as above with half the wedged lump formed into a rough cylinder about 10 in. long. Now, with your left hand outstretched, hold one end of the clay away from you and up at an angle of 45°. Rest the other end close to you on the bench.

Place your right hand on the side of the clay so that the fleshy part of the palm is halfway down. Then push down and away to the full extent of your right arm's reach. With your left hand give the clay a quarter turn and pull it back to its original angle with the bench. After several turns a spiral will develop under the right hand while under the left you should clearly see the clay folding in on itself (fig. 3).

Between 100 and 150 turns will be sufficient to get the clay into good working condition. Take care not to trap air in the final few turns: close in the spiral gradually until you are left with a rough cone shape on the bench.

2   Ox-head kneading

3   Oriental spiral kneading

Clay for all the methods of making pots described in the following pages is prepared as above. Kneading does require a little practice so don't despair if you can't get the hang of it at once. You will find it less tiring and be more efficient at it if you stand with your feet apart and rhythmically use the whole weight of your body against the clay.

Grog.   The highly plastic nature of ball clays can lead to excessive shrinking and warping of pots after they are made. To counteract this tendency a percentage of non-plastic refractory material is usually added to almost all clays except plastic porcelain bodies. This material is what potters generically call *grog*. It usually takes the form of ground fired clay which can be obtained from suppliers in various grades according to the size of mesh through which it has been passed. Fine sand can also be used as grog provided it is dug from a pit. Sand from the beach contains too many tiny particles of shell which adversely affect clays and glazes. Grog will open the clay, give it added strength, help good drying and firing, reduce shrinkage and warping and impart some texture to it.

For hand-building methods, grog can be fairly coarse and in quite high proportions up to 30%. For throwing, grog should be between 30- and 80-mesh. Coarse grog is very hard on the hands during throwing, while very fine opening material reduces plasticity considerably. Amounts in excess of 15% of any size will almost certainly reduce the plasticity of some throwing clays beyond acceptable limits.

If you use prepared plastic clay the best time to add grog is during kneading. First weigh the clay and then determine the weight of grog needed to make a particular percentage of non-plastic material. Sprinkle the grog onto the wedging bench and knead the clay over it. Gradually it will be absorbed into the mass and evenly distributed throughout it.

It is most important to keep a careful record of the proportions of grog to clay for the making of particular batches of pots. A change in the proportion will result in any new clay added to say a large coiled pot or a handle added to a thrown one shrinking at a different rate. Uneven tensions will then be set up and warping or even cracking will occur.

Adding Other Materials to Clay. The colour of clay may be modified or changed by adding small quantities of metal oxides or proprietary body stains. Obviously the paler the clay initially the greater the effect of added colour. Oxides should be used with great restraint if the resulting colour is not to be crude and harsh. More important, clay containing a high percentage of metal oxide will deform or even melt at temperatures considerably lower than would otherwise be the case. The oxide reduces refractoriness by acting as a flux. This is the reason why rich iron-bearing clays such as terra cotta vitrify at comparatively low temperatures.

To impart different textures to clay you can add small amounts of very coarse oxide or any combustible material of small particle size such as sawdust or crude wood ash. Some plasticity will inevitably by lost by doing so, but the sawdust etc. will burn away in the firing creating textures impossible to achieve by other means.

Although colouring and texturing clay can very easily degenerate into being ends in themselves there is no reason why, if used with sensitivity, they should not greatly enhance the forms you make.

Chapter 2

Hand-Built Pottery

The making of pots by hand has never been confined to the use of the potter's wheel. Splendid pots were made long before that machine was invented and in recent times we have come increasingly to appreciate the tremendous ceramic achievements of what we often, perhaps mistakenly, consider to be primitive peoples. Lacking any kind of sophisticated tools they produced pots of great aesthetic merit, subtle and generous in form, inventive and vigorous in decoration with nothing more than the clay, their bare hands and simple bonfires. Even today in many parts of the world men and especially women continue to produce outstanding examples of the potter's craft using similar simple methods. Their uninhibited delight in the use of clay is abundantly revealed in the vitality of the pots they make.

In our more technological society the work of such potters is a salutary reminder that all methods of making pots spring ultimately from that most primitive and direct one – clay held in the hands and manipulated by the fingers. This is pottery at its most intimate and immediate. In learning how to make pots ourselves it seems a good place to begin.

PINCH POTS

No method of making is simpler or more direct than holding a ball of clay in one hand and pinching it into shape with the other. For this, you should choose well-kneaded clay that is in really good plastic condition and also rather on the soft side, but not sticky. Ideally it should be as soft as possible so long as it will keep its shape without sagging.

Take a lump of clay and roll it between both hands into as near a perfect sphere as you can manage. The size of the ball is important. It should fit comfortably in the hand and for most adults a ball about the size of a small apple will be about right.

Hold the ball gently but firmly in your left hand and with the thumb of your right hand push down exactly into the centre of the ball to within a quarter of an inch of the bottom. Try to check this measurement with your fingers before proceeding further, as it is difficult to alter the base once the walls of the pot are pinched out.

Keep your right thumb in the hole you have just made and bring the four right-hand fingers to rest on the outside of the ball. Then, while slowly rotating it anti-clockwise in your left hand, pinch your thumb towards the supporting fingers to form the base of the pot (fig. 4). Feel the thickness of

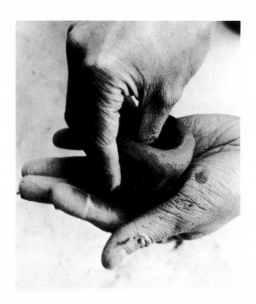

clay between your thumb and fingers and if one part seems uneven pinch there a little harder. All the time you pinch keep the ball of clay turning slowly and rhythmically in your left hand.

Once you are satisfied that the base of the pot wall is even all round, move your fingers up a little and continue squeezing and turning as before. As the walls of the pot grow taller you won't be able to get your fingers right down to the base especially if the form is slender and narrow so it is important to work from the base upwards finishing the squeezing of each bit as you go.

Pinch pots are best made quickly because holding the clay in your warm hand for any length of time will cause it to dry out and begin cracking or splitting at the rim. If this happens place the pot, rim down, on a damp sponge or cloth. This will soften the rim and after a short time you can smooth the cracks over with your finger tip and begin working again. Severe cracks are a sure sign that the clay was too stiff initially, and it is better to begin again using softer clay.

If the rim is uneven when the pot is complete cut it level with a clay trimmer. This is simply a hat pin or large needle inserted, point out, into a cork bung for a handle. Turn the pot round on its base and, starting just below the lowest point of the rim push the needle at an oblique angle into the clay. After a couple of turns the point of the needle will cut through to the inside and you can then remove the surplus.

Well-conceived and well-made pinch pots have a springing upward feeling about their shapes. To preserve this quality turn the pot on its rim to dry as soon as you have finished it. If you don't it may sag and lose much of its freshness and vitality. These two qualities distinguish good hand-made pots and any fresh touch or feeling ought to be zealously preserved.

After an hour or two – less if the room is warm – your pot will have stiffened sufficiently to retain its shape. Just before you turn it right way up give the bottom a gentle tap with the underside of a teaspoon. This will make a small concave hollow on the edge of which the pot will stand without wobbling.

With a little practice you will be able to make pinch pots quickly and in the space of an hour you should easily make several. Try and develop new and different shapes, some tall and slender, others full and rounded, turning inwards or outwards at the rim. Not all the pots need be round. When firm enough to turn right way up you can carefully and gradually beat them into a variety of geometric or asymmetric shapes using a flat or textured piece of wood.

Joined Pinch Pots. Although usually small in scale pinch pots are not as limited in size as one might suppose. Larger pots can be made by joining two or more together. The size and shape of the pots to be joined can be different, but it is important that the diameter of their rims is the same.

Having made two pinch pots trim the tops level with a needle and invert them on the bench. Decide which pot is to be the bottom one of the two and tap the concave hollow base of this with a spoon. As soon as the pots are stiff enough to hold their shapes without sagging turn them right way up. Score both the rims lightly and rub slip on the rim of one. (When slip is used for joining clay to clay it should be very thick and sticky – the consistency of stiff honey. If it is too thin the parts to be joined will slide instead of gripping.) Join the pots together scored rim to rim giving a very gentle twist as you do it so that they really bite one against the other. Then, very carefully to avoid trapping air between the rims, smooth the joint with your finger or a wooden tool. In what was originally the base of the upper pot cut a hole and pinch the clay to form a rim. Or, if you wish, continue building by adding another pot as before (fig. 5).

5 Joining pinch pots

6   Group of pinched and rolled pots

Rolled Pinch Pots.   You can have a lot of fun with pinch pots by joining two carefully together and rolling the new shape, still totally enclosed, on the bench. The air trapped inside the pot will prevent it from collapsing, and while it can change its shape it cannot alter its volume. By rocking and rolling in different directions the form can be altered until it seems satisfying. It is a random method, but the exciting and often unpredictable results are very appealing.

At their best these pinched and rolled pots have something of the character of pebbles on the beach. They can be enriched by incising, combing or glazing part of the surface.

It is essential before they pass the 'leather-hard' stage – i.e. when the clay is really firm but you can still impress a finger nail in it – that a small unobtrusive hole is cut in rolled pots. Without this, as the clay dries and shrinks it will compress air inside the pot and if it doesn't fracture on finally drying it is likely to explode on heating in the kiln (fig. 6).

COIL POTS
Joining coils of clay to form pots has obvious affinities with basket making, and pottery may well have evolved from that craft. Much early pottery was decorated by marks closely resembling basket weaves, and baskets certainly play a part in speculation about the origins of pottery. It is often thought

31

the discovery that clay could be made permanent by heat came about by the accidental burning of baskets lined with clay.

Coiling is a method which offers scope for working on a larger scale. The size of pots you can make is determined only by the size of your kiln and not even by that, for it is an easy matter today to join fired pieces very satisfactorily, using modern epoxy resin adhesives.

Coiling needs practice before it becomes rhythmic and controlled, but with a little experience you should find pots made in this way growing steadily. It is not as slow a method as one might suppose, and it combines very well with other ways of hand-building. Above all it affords the most time for study and contemplation of the forms you are creating. It is, in fact, a very peaceful and restful technique.

Although not impossible, the making of small domestic ware by coiling does require especial skill and sensitivity, and such domestic pots are better thrown. While the wheel precludes the making of other than round forms coiling is free from this limitation. The making of asymmetrical shapes is, therefore, one of its greatest advantages. When coiling concentrate on larger pots such as flower containers, bowls, lamp bases, bottles or sculptural forms, attempting shapes which could never be made on a wheel no matter how great your throwing skill. A common fault with beginners' coiled pots is that they have the semblance of thrown shapes without the spontaneity and vigour so characteristic of that technique.

For coiling an open clay is best. Add a percentage of grog or sand or both up to a maximum of about 20% (1 part grog to 4 parts dry clay or 1 part grog to 7 parts prepared clay, allowing for the moisture content of the latter). Very large coil pots will need to be fairly thick, say half an inch, to support their own weight during making. For these, use grog which is fairly coarse in particle size, 30-mesh or less. However dry a pot may seem before firing it still contains a proportion of water. The addition of grog helps to create passage ways in the clay body through which this moisture can escape on firing. Obviously the thicker the wall of the pot the more moisture it contains and hence the larger the escape passages need to be.

Prepare sufficient clay at a time. All the pottery we use in our daily lives for eating and drinking is so light and comparatively small that it can come as a surprise just how much clay is needed to make a large pot. In any case having to stop to knead more clay can be frustrating and something of the precious rhythm of the work can easily be lost as a consequence. Any surplus can easily be stored in polythene for another working session. If you do this be sure to put a label in with the clay stating the proportions of the grog/clay mix. In this way, even if you come back to it weeks later, you will know for certain what it is. It seems only common sense to do this but occasionally I have myself thought 'I'll remember that', and have not bothered to label clays and glazes. I have nearly always had cause to regret the omission!

You will probably have to move a coil pot around in the course of construction so before you begin find a small board or tile which will be easily portable on which you can build the pot. The slightly absorbant unglazed side of a 6 in tile is a good surface because the clay will not stick readily to it. But sprinkling a board with fine sand or powdered flint will serve equally well. A banding wheel, a kind of stable circular platform which turns on a stand, is a great help when you are coiling but it is not essential.

To make the base take a lump of clay, place it on the sanded board or on the tile and pat it into a flat disc with the palm of your hand until it is half an inch thick. Alternatively roll it out with a rolling pin. If the base is to be round take anything circular you can find – a cup, bowl or can – of the size you want, impress it lightly into the clay and cut round the mark with a sharp knife. Asymmetrical bases can be cut freehand.

The next step is to make the coils. Take a double handful of clay, or as much as you can manage, and squeeze it into a rough coil. Place this on the bench and roll it until it is an even thickness along its length. Start in the middle and work outwards gently and evenly, using the flat fingers and palms. There is no need to press hard; let the weight of the clay do most of the work.

After rolling beat the clay flat with the fleshy part of the hand. Then turn it over and beat the other side. Do this on another part of the bench, otherwise it will stick (fig. 7).

Don't roll or beat the coils too thin because if the wall of the pot is not sufficiently thick to begin with you will have difficulty in controlling the shape. In extreme cases the pot may even collapse under its own weight. Make a few coils at a time so you don't lose the rhythm of the work by having to stop and make more.

The first coil is put directly onto the edge of the base. Hold one end up in your left hand and the other in your right. Place the right hand end onto the edge of the base and join it firmly by pressing down with the thumb. There is no need to score the base or use slip for joining at this stage. Move along the coil pressing the inside edge of it onto the base as you go. Note that the coil is not laid round the base and then joined to it, but put on and

7 Preparing coils

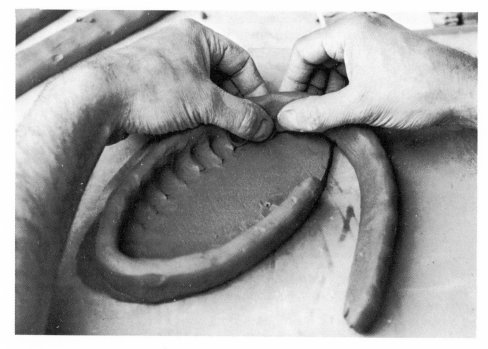

joined *all in one movement* (fig. 8). If you don't do this the pot always grows outwards as well as upwards because the coil expands in length as it is pressed down.

Join the next and subsequent coils by laying them on the top of the one below and thumbing down first the inside and then the outside. Take care that air is not trapped in the joints. Pay particular attention to the places where the coil rejoins itself and remember to stagger these joins round the circumference of the pot. Placing them immediately above one another will result in a vertical weakness down its edge. To make the pot grow vertically place each coil on the centre of the one below. Inward and outward shaping is done by using coils previously bent into a curve on the bench. By doing this you make the two edges of the coil a different length. For inward shaping the longer outer curve of the coil is the one joined to the pot and for outward shaping the shorter inward edge goes down first. The amount of curve in the coil will determine the degree of inward or outward movement of the pot shape.

Smooth off the inside of the pot as completely as you can while it is being built and keep the wall of even thickness (fig. 9). Don't hesitate to pinch the form using both hands or to fill in any hollows or weaknesses with small pieces of clay.

After two or three coils step back and consider the shape and profile from different angles. If you think the form needs altering in any way now is the time to do it. While the clay is still soft and plastic you can change the shape

9   Smoothing the coils. See how the left hand supports the clay

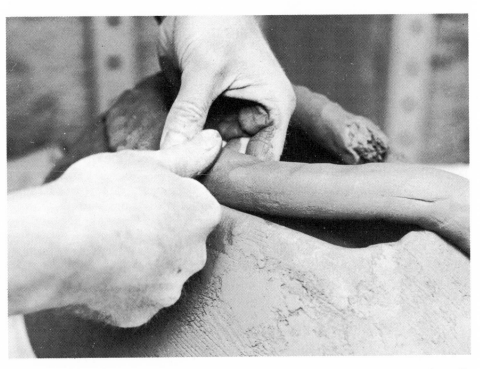

10   Thumbing down one of the last few coils

by beating the outside with a flat piece of wood say 2 in by 1 in. For beating inside a large wooden spoon is ideal for the job. Be quite bold over this beating because once the pot is leather hard the only way you can alter the shape is by scraping away clay from the outside of the wall. Obviously this can result in parts of the pot being thinner than others.

Tops and rims need particular consideration and care. They are the potter's final statement before he leaves off making. The tops of many beginner's pots are seldom given sufficient emphasis: too often they have the air of being abandoned rather than finished. Emphasis may be subtle or dramatic but it should be definite. Thin tops look especially weak on a large pot. To achieve a crisp, finished look the top ought to be at least as thick as the rest of the pot and possibly a little more. You will find it helpful where a shape diminishes towards the top to decrease the thickness of the last two or three coils (fig. 10). It can also help if, before you put these on, the rim is levelled off with a trimmer. For small diameter pots you can proceed as for pinch pots, but for larger ones use the trimmer just to score the clay and then remove the surplus by cutting carefully round with a thin-bladed knife. Complete the pot by smoothing the outside. A piece of old hacksaw blade is an excellent tool for this. Use the toothed edge first to remove any bumps, then with the other edge smooth the surface of the pot. You can, of course, leave it textured if you prefer. The large coil pot by Geoffrey Doonan (colour plate 7) was decorated in this way. The surface was first scraped with a piece of wood-shaping tool blade. Oxides and a dry matt glaze were later rubbed into parts of the surface to emphasise the pattern. Finally, turn the pot over and give a slight undercut to the base. The line of dark shadow cast by this bevel greatly helps to give the pot the appearance of sitting firmly.

Larger Coiled Forms. With larger coiled forms you may be able to build only part of the pot at a time. If any sagging occurs it is a sign that the clay below is too soft to support the weight of clay above. You should, therefore, leave off and put the pot aside to stiffen. It helps to keep the rhythm of work going if you build two or three pots at a time, working on one while the others are stiffening. A sheet of polythene or a damp cloth placed round the top will keep just the rim soft while the lower part dries a little. In this way new coils can be added later without danger of cracking at the joint.

Very large rounded forms with narrow necks, such as the one by Geoffrey Doonan described above, are best made in two stages. The first is to coil an inverted bowl shape which is then allowed to stiffen. In the second stage this shape is turned right way up and the top half of the pot coiled on it. The form is, in effect, made from the middle towards first the base and then the top.

Fig. 11 shows how this kind of pot is begun. Place a curved coil, long edge down, on a damp cloth and coil the shape up and in towards what will eventually be the base. Close the form right in and then gently beat the top of it flat to make the base. Now leave the form to dry a little, but place a

11 Beginning a large
round coiled form

damp cloth around the bottom of it to keep the rim soft for adding new clay.

When the form is stiff enough to hold its shape, reverse it and score the rim. Add further coils as before gradually closing in the shape until the pot is completed.

At the end of a working session unfinished pots can be kept damp and soft by covering them completely with sheets of polythene tied with string. It is important to exclude all air, so tuck the ends of the sheet firmly under the board or tile the pot stands on. If the pot is to be left for longer than three or four days, place damp, but not wet, cloths over it before covering with polythene.

SLAB-BUILT POTS

Clay Preparation. Slabs of clay rolled out flat, cut to shape and joined afford enormous scope for hand-building from simple tiles to complex and precise forms. Slab-building lacks perhaps the intimacy and immediacy of pinch pots and coiling, but it has advantages in other directions. It enables you to make very angular forms impossible by other methods; work can be carefully planned in advance, making results perhaps more certain, and the large flat areas involved lend themselves especially to the decorative treatment of clay surfaces. Slab-building combines well with throwing or coiling, the angularity of the one contrasting with and complementing the roundness of the others.

Whether you decide to make tiles, hollow forms or press moulded dishes from slabs of clay the principal difficulty you will encounter is how to prevent the clay from warping as it is dried and fired. Industrially this is overcome, in the manufacture of tiles for example, by moulding damp clay powder under great pressure. But the equipment needed for this is quite outside the scope of the hand potter, who must solve the problems of making flat objects by using clay incorporating the maximum amount of non-plastic material.

37

The preparation and joining of slabs puts less strain on clay than other methods. No pinching or beating is involved and it is possible, therefore, to add more sand or grog than for coiling, for instance. With a good clay up to 30% can be added without excessive loss of plasticity. The more non-plastic material you can incorporate into the clay the less its shrinkage and the fewer chances of warping – which is really distortion brought about by local and hence uneven shrinkage.

Any sand or grog ought to be on the coarse side for slab-building or tiles. Between 20- and 40-mesh is the most suitable. Don't have the clay too stiff, and wedge and knead it particularly well: once the clay has been rolled flat it is difficult to remove air bubbles.

If only a few slabs are needed the easiest way of preparing them is to use a rolling pin to flatten the clay out on a cloth with a slight textured surface such as hessian or coarse calico. This enables you to free the clay from the bench at the appropriate time.

At opposite edges of the cloth place two thin strips of wood about 1 in wide and the required thickness of the slab to act as rolling guides. Very thin slabs warp more easily than thicker ones so the guides should be not less than $\frac{1}{4}$ in thick. Large pots and dishes will need slabs $\frac{3}{8}$ in or $\frac{5}{8}$ in thick.

Place a lump of clay in the middle of the cloth between the guides and with the palm of your hand beat it as flat as you can. Turn it over two or three times to avoid wrinkles in the clay and the cloth. Then, after checking that the cloth is smooth and flat, roll the clay until the ends of the rolling pin are resting on the guides (fig. 12). From time to time you may need to cut

12 Rolling clay between guides for making tiles and slab-built pots

off any surplus clay which prevents this from happening. If the clay sticks to the rolling pin lightly dust it with powdered flint or quartz.

Larger quantities of slabs are better cut from a block of clay. Cut notches in two sticks $\frac{1}{2}$ in $\times \frac{3}{4}$ in at $\frac{1}{4}$ in, $\frac{3}{8}$ in or $\frac{1}{2}$ in intervals. Hardwood is best. Place a large, well-kneaded lump of clay on the bench and beat it into a rectangular block. Fix a wire only a little wider than the block between the lowest two notches on the sticks. Pull the wire as taut as possible between the sticks and draw it towards you through the block of clay keeping the ends of the sticks firmly on the bench. Successive slabs are cut from the same block by simply moving the wire up the sticks one notch at a time. When the block is cut remove the slabs carefully and place them on textured cloth or lightly sanded board to stiffen. The wire will invariably drag coarse pieces of grog across the slabs and score the surface. They may be smoothed with a kidney-shaped rubber smoothing tool obtainable from suppliers, or left as a textured surface.

TILES

Hand-made tiles should not be too thin or too large if they are to dry and fire reasonably flat. A tile 2 in $\times$ 2 in should not be less than $\frac{1}{4}$ in thick and for 6 in $\times$ 6 in tiles $\frac{3}{8}$ in to $\frac{5}{8}$ in thick would be appropriate. Tiles in excess of 6 in $\times$ 6 in are very difficult to make satisfactorily by hand, and even with smaller sizes it may be impossible to achieve the flatness of tiles made industrially.

Roll the clay out as described above onto a lightly sanded board instead of on a cloth. Measure carefully the size of tile you want, bearing in mind that the fired size will be approximately $\frac{1}{10}$ less because of shrinkage. Cut the tiles to size using a thin sharp knife held vertically against a ruler. Any decorating of tiles by impressed pattern should be done before cutting otherwise they will distort as objects are pressed into the clay. For making tiles in quantity it is worthwhile purchasing a tile cutter. This is a sharp-

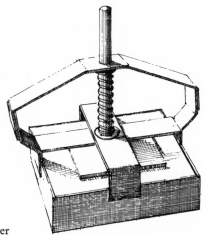

13   A tile cutter

edged metal mould in which is located a spring loaded plunger (fig. 13). After cutting, the tile is gently pressed from the mould by the plunger without distortion. Various shapes and sizes of cutter are available from potter's merchants and suppliers.

Great care must be taken in drying tiles. Avoid strong draughts or heat and turn the tiles frequently on their boards so that they have every chance to dry and contract slowly and evenly. Lastly make sure that the kiln shelf on which they are fired is perfectly flat or all your efforts will have been in vain. At stoneware temperatures particularly pots very readily distort to the shape of the shelf on which they are fired.

Another method of making successful flat tiles involves cutting down the percentage of grog and substituting 15–20% of a quick-setting refractory cement, with the result that the tiles set flat before they are fully dry. Some builders' merchants stock this kind of cement. It may cause the clay to darken considerably, but this colour disappears on firing. Speed of making is essential and any surplus clay containing cement must be discarded, and not allowed to contaminate other clays. NOTE: Only specially prepared refractory cements are at all suitable for this method. *Ordinary cements should on no account be used.*

SLAB-BUILDING

As an introduction to slab-building, simple and easy pots can be made by folding clay round any cylindrical object provided that it isn't too large or its curve too acute. The various sizes of cardboard cylinders used for packaging are ideal, or even the rolling pin with which you roll out the clay. The only difficulty will be freeing the cylinder from the clay on completion of the pot. To do this, fold a piece of paper round the cylinder you plan to use as a forma (i.e., support) for the pot and secure the edges with transparent tape. The clay will adhere only to the paper inside which the forma will slide easily.

Roll out the clay on a cloth as described above and cut a strip as wide as the height of the pot and longer than the circumference of the cylinder. Place the forma on one end of the strip and fold the clay round it. Either cut where the edges meet or make a decorative feature of the joint. Smooth the seam carefully with your finger or a wooden tool. Make any impressed decoration with the forma still inside. Then withdraw the support.

Roll and cut a base to size. Score the end of the pot and the edges of the base. Rub thick slip into the score marks and join the base and pot together with a gentle twisting action. Carefully smooth the joint.

The disadvantage of pots made in this way are aesthetic rather than practical. Angular forms are more in keeping with the method of slab construction and like some coiled pots, round slab-built ones seem clumsy and heavy in comparison with thrown counterparts. But it is an easy way of beginning to learn slab-building – especially for younger children who will not have developed, perhaps, the patience and perseverence needed for constructing angular forms.

Angular Forms.   Angular slab-built pots can be thought of as an extension of tile making in that they are constructed by joining several slabs or tiles together.

Roll out on a cloth at least a quarter inch thickness of clay or more depending on the size of the pot. Have a plan of its shape in mind before you begin cutting the slabs. Remember that the overlap where the walls of the pot join will affect the final shape. Either measure the base and sides as for tiles or, if several similar sized pots are planned, it is worthwhile making cardboard templates. Impress any pattern before cutting.

Cut the slabs out holding a knife vertically against a ruler, lift the cloth and very gingerly pull them away avoiding distortion as much as you can. Place the cut shapes on a lightly sanded board and leave them to stiffen.

As soon as they will retain their shape they are ready for joining. This may be earlier than you think because two slabs will stand joined together without distortion where one won't.

The point of structural weakness in any slab pot is obviously at the joints. Successful pots must, therefore, be assembled with care. Mitring the corners by cutting adjacent edges at an angle of 45° gives both the maximum joining area and the greatest control over the shape. It is also the most trouble, and if you don't have the patience for this you can join the pieces by placing an end on top of an edge.

Begin by putting the largest slab with the greatest length (which may not necessarily be the base) at the bottom so that the pot has maximum support. For a simple rectangular pot join the slabs in this sequence:

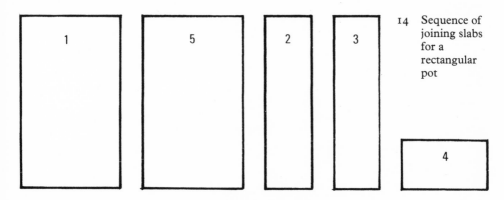

14   Sequence of joining slabs for a rectangular pot

To join the slabs score all the surfaces where the slabs will meet. (This will, incidentally, give you a good idea of the state of the clay: if it seems on the stiff side damp the surfaces with a sponge.) Rub thick slip into the score marks. Then press the two edges together with a firm but gentle sawing action so they really bite one against the other. Smooth the outside of the joint with a finger or wooden tool.

On the inside angle add a small thin coil of clay. Start in the middle and press the coil well into the angle making sure that no air is trapped (fig. 15).

41

15 Pressing a small coil of clay into the angle of a slab pot

16 Adding the final slab

Work out towards each end thumbing the coil onto both adjacent surfaces. This coil will both strengthen the joint and prevent the corners from being thinner and weaker than the rest of the pot should you decide to remove the sharp outer edge. Clay is not a material that lends itself to very acute angles and the appearance of slab pots is nearly always improved by some slight softening of edges.

When you come to join the base (piece no. 4 in fig. 14), place it over and not into the other three pieces so that you can see all the joints. The small coils adjacent to the last piece (no. 5 in the diagram) must be put in place after the pot has been assembled (fig. 16).

Larger Slab Pots.   Slabs needed for larger pots will probably be too hard to effect a satisfactory joint if they are left to stiffen until they can hold their shape. They must, therefore, be joined before this stage and supported during the actual construction.

Bricks or blocks of wood give good outside support while crumpled newspaper or thin cardboard cartons can be used inside. Newspaper may be left to burn away in the firing, but any rigid inside support pieces ought to be withdrawn as soon as possible. If left in too long the drying clay will shrink against them and crack.

17   A group of simple slab-built pots

PRESS-MOULDED DISHES

Flat slabs of clay pressed into or over moulds present particular opportunities for decorating large flat areas of clay, together with the chance of making shallow oval, rectangular or asymmetric shapes. Circular dishes can also be formed in this way but they are much more quickly made and have more life and vigour if thrown on a wheel.

Making moulded dishes involves two distinct processes:

1. the making of the mould itself from a clay model; and

2. the pressing of a slab of clay either into or over the mould to make the finished dish.

Moulds are semi-permanent and can be used repeatedly, and there are two kinds you can make: *hump* moulds over which the clay is first draped and then smoothed and cut to shape, and *drop* moulds into which the clay is pressed and the rim later trimmed to size. Which of the two you choose depends mainly on the shape of the dish and the method of decorating it. Hump moulds are more appropriate for shallow shapes; drop moulds are generally used for deeper dishes and for techniques involving impressed or slipped decoration where the clay needs greater support. The making of both kinds of mould begins in a similar way.

Making the Model. The model for the mould is made upside down from a solid mass of well-grogged and well-kneaded clay placed on a flat surface such as a piece of plywood or hardboard (Masonite).

Decide first on the shape of the dish. Then from stiff paper cut two templates, one to the shape and size of the rim, the other to the shape and size of the base. Avoid shapes with sharp corners, right angles and any undercutting. Square and rectangular dishes should have their corners slightly rounded to avoid straining the clay unduly at these points. To get all the corners the same shape fold the paper in four before cutting.

Rim and base templates for oval dishes may be drawn as follows: roughly in the centre of a piece of paper fix two small nails a few inches apart. Make a loop of thin string and tie a pencil on it at any point. Place the loop over the nails, extend it to its fullest extent and move the pencil around the two centres, making sure that you keep the pencil vertical at all times. Different ovals can be made by adjusting either the distance between the two nails or by the length of the loop, or both. It is also a great help if you cut a template for the profile of the dish. A thick cardboard template will be sufficient to test the profile shape from time to time, but if you use thin plywood you can use the template itself to scrape and shape the clay.

To make the model, lay the rim template on the flat surface and cover it with clay. The lump should be sufficient to both cover the template completely and also be a little higher than you wish the dish to be deep. Flatten the lump and place the base template in the centre of the clay. Then cut and beat it to the desired shape of the dish. Use both shape templates as guides. Finally smooth the model with a rubber kidney.

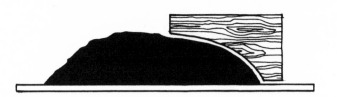

Drop Moulds are cast in plaster-of-Paris from the model. Good casting requires swift action, so have everything to hand including extra plaster and water if needed.

When the model is leather hard build a wall round it to contain the plaster using waste clay or pieces of wood. This needs to be about one and a half inches higher than the model and two or three inches away from it. Support the wall with bricks if necessary. Plug any gaps with clay.

Use fine potter's plaster and mix it as follows. Fill a plastic bowl or bucket two thirds with water. Sprinkle plaster into it until it appears above the surface. Always add the plaster to the water and not vice versa. Stir the plaster gently with one hand so that all air rises to the surface. Keep the other hand dry for adding more plaster if necessary, until the mixture reaches the point at which it begins noticeably to stiffen.

Now you must move swiftly. Just before the plaster begins to set pour it quickly over the clay model until it is level with the top of the retaining wall. Then tilt the hardboard and bang it two or three times to level the plaster. If you find you haven't mixed enough score the surface of the plaster already over the model, quickly mix more and pour in.

It is very important to add sufficient plaster to the water so that the mix almost reaches setting point before pouring. Adding less to the mix certainly slows the setting speed and gives more time for pouring, but it also makes a very soft and friable plaster which rapidly becomes sodden in use and which lacks durability. This fact should also be closely observed when making plaster slabs on which reclaimed clay is to be dried.

Within a few minutes of pouring, the plaster will set hard and become quite warm. After half an hour it is safe to remove the retaining walls. You can then turn the mould over, pull away the hardboard and dig out the expendable clay model. You now have a drop mould. Clean up the edges of the rim with a sharp knife and leave to dry thoroughly before using.

Hump Moulds are cast from drop moulds and several can be made successively if required using the drop mould as a master. Begin by building a wall of clay about an inch high round the rim of the drop mould. To prevent the casting from sticking, coat the inside of the mould with a soft soap such as washing-up liquid, or with corn oil. Plaster is very absorbent and it will need several applications before a definite coating has built up on the surface.

Mix plaster-of-Paris as above and pour it into the mould until it is level with the top of the clay wall. Before the plaster sets hard push an old pot or

45

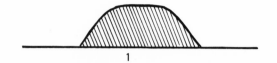

1

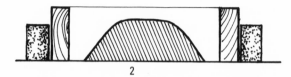

2

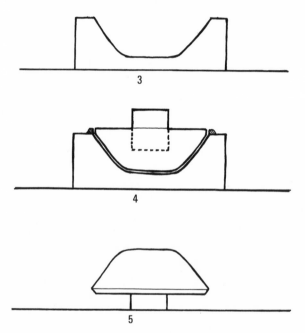

3

4

5

19 Stages in making dish moulds:
1 Clay model;
2 Drop mould cast up-side down over clay model;
3 Drop mould right way up, clay model removed;
4 Hump mould cast up-side down in drop mould, tin can or pot pushed into plaster just before it sets;
5 Hump mould removed ready for use.

tin can into it but not through it. This addition will provide a stand to lift the mould off the bench when in use. Bang the mould to level the plaster and leave to set hard.

If you have put sufficient soap or oil between the moulds they should come apart easily. In case of difficulty immersing them in water nearly always parts them. Finally when the hump mould is dry cut a bevel at 45° from the rim.

A brief word of caution about plaster-of-Paris. Store it in a dry place and preferably in an air-tight container. Plaster is hygroscopic: it absorbs moisture from the atmosphere and becomes lumpy and virtually unusable as a result. For this reason never put a wet hand in it. Always use one hand for stirring and the other for scooping. *Never* throw plaster down sinks – its capacity for blocking drains is outstanding. And don't hesitate to discard any clay contaminated by plaster.

Making the Dish.   Prepare clay as for slab pots, rolling out well-kneaded, well-grogged clay between rolling guides on a textured cloth. The sloping sides of pressed dishes take more clay than you might first realise, so check that the slab is sufficient to more than cover the mould.

FOR HUMP MOULDS,   gently place the mould upside down in the centre of the clay. Lift the cloth together with both the clay and the mould and smartly turn the mould so that it stands right way up on the bench. For large dishes you may need someone to help you do this. Smooth, but don't press, the cloth to ensure that the clay follows closely the shape of the mould. Now peel off the cloth carefully. You can either leave the pleasant texture left by the cloth or smooth the clay with a rubber kidney. Then cut off surplus clay with a short wire or small harp following the bevelled rim. Work from the centre of each side towards the corners to avoid distorting the shape of the latter.

As the dish dries it will shrink away from the mould. When it is leather hard and will hold its shape – and not before, or it will surely warp – lift it carefully from the mould. Now give careful consideration to the rim, smoothing and shaping it so that there are no sharp edges. We nearly always view a shallow dish from above, seldom seeing the profile. The rim is, therefore, a dominant feature, always in our eye containing and delineating the form. Any unevenness or careless finishing of rims appears, in consequence, to be magnified.

FOR DROP MOULDS,   placing the clay is a bit trickier than for hump moulds, and speed is essential. Prepare the slab of clay as before, then lift the cloth with the clay attached to it and hold it vertically over the mould. Grasp one end of the cloth holding the clay onto it with the fingers of both hands and lay the other end against the nearer edge of the mould. Lower the clay away from you so that it covers the whole mould and then carefully peel the cloth away.

Now take the edge of the clay and ease it further into the mould until the base of the dish is firmly supported. Pinch off the more obviously surplus clay from round the rim. Then press the clay closely against the mould, beginning in the centre of the base and working outwards. Use only a rubber kidney for this: a damp sponge is unsatisfactory, and the pressure of your fingers will leave distinct marks difficult to eradicate. Ensure that the clay is firmly pressed into the angle between the base and the walls of the dish and in the corners. Finally trim the edge level with a wire or harp (a U-shaped metal or wooden tool, across the ends of which is stretched a cutting wire), again pulling from the centre of the sides towards the corners.

Any decoration with slip should be done immediately after making.

Pour in sufficient to cover the base and then tilt the mould from side to side so that slip covers the whole surface. Pour out the surplus, holding the edges of the clay securely as you do so. When the slip has dried a little, ease the clay from the edge of the mould by following the rim with the point of a sharp knife or clay trimmer. Cutting down no more than $\frac{1}{2}$ in between the edge of the clay and the mould will be sufficient to allow the dish to shrink freely in the mould as it dries. When the dish has shrunk and is leather hard and stiff remove it from the mould and give a final finish to the rim.

There are uneven tensions in press-moulded dishes because of their shape, and once freed from their mould they should be slowly and carefully dried. Contrary to what one might think, I have always found less distortion takes place in the fire if dishes are dried the right way up.

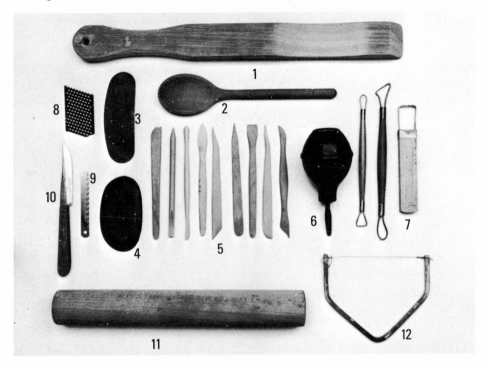

20 Tools for hand-building and decorating:

1 Clay beater	5 Boxwood modelling tools	9 Piece of broken hack saw blade
2 Wooden spoon	6 Slip trailer	10 Kitchen knife
3 Metal kidney	7 Wire loop modelling tools	11 Rolling pin
4 Rubber kidney	8 Piece of broken shaping tool blade	12 Harp

Chapter 3

Throwing

No one who stands by his wheel and watches a skilled potter throwing can fail to be fascinated by the way in which the spinning clay swells and grows under his hands. From a shapeless lump the clay is transformed into a hollow pot in what seems but a matter of moments. Of all the methods of making pots by hand the potter's wheel uniquely combines something of the speed and precision of a machine without in any way denying the potter full opportunity for creative and inventive expression. However swiftly and regularly pots are thrown none has the dead uniformity of those made by machine alone. Each thrown pot bears the imprint of the hand – and the mind – of the potter who made it, and thus each pot retains some life and vitality of its own.

As with any skill, some people take to throwing more readily than others. The basic principles are not hard to grasp and it should not be long before you have some success, but real proficiency does require long practice and experience. The skilled potter makes the job of throwing seem deceptively easy, the pots almost flow from the wheelhead. But what the spectator never sees, of course, is the amount of time spent in achieving that high degree of skill. Throwing is not made easier by having inadequate equipment, and great attention, therefore, should be given to the choice of both wheels and clays.

CHOOSING A WHEEL

A potter's wheel of any kind should first and foremost be robust and solidly constructed, so that it is free from any vibration when in use. All working parts ought to be easily accessible, and in particular there should be accessible greasing points for each bearing.

The tray in which slops and clay turnings collect ought to be sufficiently large to avoid frequent emptying. Some wheels have removable trays and these are particularly useful if you want to change to a different clay without the trouble of thoroughly cleaning out a fixed tray. There should in any case be a good wide drain in the base of the tray and an overflow in one side of it. The purpose of the latter is to prevent water entering and damaging the top bearings: it should, therefore, always be kept free from obstruction. Wheels should also have generous provision at the edge of the tray for balls of prepared clay, a water bowl, tools and a board for finished pots. If a seat is provided it should, ideally, slope forward slightly, and its front edge ought not to be more than about 8 in or 10 in from the centre of the wheelhead for a comfortable working position. Wheelheads themselves are made of cast iron or aluminium alloy, and either screw or taper into a vertical shaft attached to the drive. Various sizes are interchangeable, but if you are going to have only one choose as large a size as the tray will allow.

A very wide range of kick (foot operated) and electric wheels is available from suppliers, or you may be able to buy one second-hand.

Kick Wheels are much cheaper to buy, cost nothing to run and are virtually silent in use. More important, from the point of view of quality of work, they are more sensitive, responding far quicker than an electric motor to slight changes of speed within the making of a single pot. With a kick wheel, therefore, you have greater control. You are in direct contact not only with the clay but also with the instrument of making itself.

All kick wheels incorporate a flywheel in their design, which ensures a smooth action, especially at low speeds. The momentum of the flywheel also prevents fatigue. Its weight, therefore, is of paramount importance. If it is too light, centring clay rapidly becomes hard work and steadiness is lost at low speeds when pots are being finished. If it is too heavy, starting and stopping the wheel are difficult and tiring and the making of each pot takes longer than it need. Flywheels weighing between 30 and 60 lb will be found to be the most satisfactory.

The flywheel revolves by kicking a treadle bar with the left leg, and it is important that this treadle can be adjusted for various leg lengths.

Above all there should be a seat on which you can sit comfortably while you throw. Some suppliers offer cheap kick wheels without seats and with the treadle at the front instead of at the side. They are a false economy and one can only assume that they have been designed by people with no knowledge of throwing. To operate them it is necessary to be a kind of ceramic Nureyev, balancing on one leg while kicking with the other. Anyone learning to throw can do without this quite unnecessary handicap.

Some potters prefer kick wheels without a treadle at all. They work by sitting and rhythmically kicking the flywheel itself. Such kick wheels are very simple, but their use does require greater skill and co-ordination than the treadle type.

Electric Wheels. Of those available, the best kind are those powered by a D.C. motor which gives greater torque and lower speeds than the more usual A.C. motor driven ones. All electric wheels have a foot switch to vary the speed of rotation and this should not be so sensitive that increases and decreases of speed are too violent. The speed range of electric wheels is important. They should have a minimum speed of not more than 30 r.p.m. and a maximum of not less than 150 r.p.m. The speed should be infinitely variable between minimum and maximum, and not just a pre-set series. The motor should also have sufficient power so that it is impossible to stop the rotation by applying pressure to any reasonable weight of clay. Some cheap electric wheels are very poor in this respect. It is possible to throw standing up using electric wheels, but if a seat is incorporated it should be comfortable and capable of adjustment for varying leg lengths.

It is, I think, important to realise that the extra cost of buying and running an electric wheel only really absolves you from the task of kicking round the wheel yourself. Except perhaps in the case of very large pots I don't think electric wheels make the actual job of throwing much easier. The quality of the shapes you make and the speed at which you make them depend far more on your own skill and experience.

CLAY FOR THROWING

Throwing demands more of a clay than any other method of making. To withstand the strains and stresses of being formed quickly a good throwing clay needs to be highly plastic, but not so plastic that it becomes what potters call 'soapy', that is covered in thick slip while being worked. It should also be rigid enough when wet to retain the shape imposed on it. Some plastic clays collapse suddenly because of a critical water absorbency rate, and these should be avoided.

Many red earthenware and ball clays and some plastic fireclays make excellent throwing bodies. Their working properties are improved if they are opened up with 10–15% of grog or fine sand. This gives the wet clay some rigidity and reduces high shrinkage which is a common feature of very plastic clays. Between 30- and 80-mesh is the best size for grog or sand in throwing bodies. Coarse grog is especially hard on the hands and very fine grog robs the clay of much of the plasticity essential for throwing.

You will certainly find that a good clay makes learning to throw much easier. When you are beginning it is worthwhile trying several different clays at first. Then, having found one that seems satisfactory, keep to it until you have gained some knowledge of what it will do for you.

Much of the difficulty encountered in learning to throw can be reduced or eliminated by using clay of the right condition and consistency. When throwing, the clay is formed by even pressure of the hands and any unevenness in the clay invariably results in eccentric and wobbly shapes which quickly collapse.

It is essential, then, that clay intended for throwing is well wedged and kneaded to render it completely homogenous and as free as possible from air pockets. Clay rapidly becomes hard on the outside if it is left on an absorbent surface or in a warm atmosphere, and it ought to be used at once after preparation. Any clay not required immediately should be kept soft by carefully wrapping it in polythene. Many beginners have the clay too stiff, which makes centring difficult and which often leads to pots of uneven thickness. Very new clay is unsuitable for throwing: its shortness (i.e., lack of plasticity) leads to pots splitting at the rim.

Prepare plenty of clay at a time. Throwing is essentially a repetitive process and skill comes more quickly if you can have long and uninterrupted attempts at mastering the techniques.

TOOLS

Tools for throwing are very simple and cheap. They are best kept conveniently to hand on a board or shelf attached to the wheel. You will need:

1. A bowl of water to lubricate the clay during throwing. It should be of a generous size so that you don't need to fill it too often.

2. A small sponge of fine to medium texture about 4 in long and $2\frac{1}{2}$ in wide. Natural sponges are best.

3. A clay knife made from a piece of wood about 5 in or 6 in long by $\frac{3}{4}$ in wide and $\frac{1}{4}$ in thick. It should be sharpened to a chisel edge at both ends at an angle of 45°. Box-wood knives are satisfactory but a piece of bamboo is best. It is very hard and wears well. In use the knife is self-sharpening.

4. A clay trimmer made from a large needle fixed into a cork for a handle.

5. Three or four cutting wires with handles. These are used to free pots from the wheelhead and their length varies with the size of pot being made. You will need a very short one about 3 in or 4 in for some kinds of lids, and a long one about 16 in or 18 in for flat plates and dishes. 8–10 in is a good length for general use.

6. A pair of calipers for measuring the diameters of lids etc. Rust-proof aluminium or plastic ones with an adjustable wing nut are the best to use. Calipers capable of spans up to 20–24 in will be sufficient for almost any sized pot.

7. A selection of various sized batts on which to throw larger pots. Their use is described later in this section.

8. A number of ware boards about 7 in or 8 in wide by 30 in or 36 in long on which you can place newly thrown pots. They can also be used as drying shelves and for carrying pots to the kiln.

THROWING

Throughout all the stages of throwing it is important to be comfortable and relaxed. Physical tension is an enemy of good throwing. It inhibits rhythmic kicking and smooth hand actions and leads to early fatigue. Kicking with the ball of the foot on the treadle rather than with the instep greatly helps to maintain a smooth kicking action. Beginners will also find it helpful to sit at the wheel and accustom themselves to the movement of their leg and the wheel before using any clay. With practice, kicking becomes automatic. Almost all kick wheels have the treadle on the left and the pots are pulled up on the right to balance the body. The wheel should revolve in an *anti-clockwise* direction. All electric wheels revolve anti-clockwise.

Centring. The first stage of throwing is to press the ball of clay into the dead centre of the wheel so that when the ball is hollowed out the walls of the growing pot will be of even thickness in section and the rim level.

Beginners will find a ball of clay weighing about 1 lb or $1\frac{1}{2}$ lb the most comfortable size to start with. Have your water bowl, sponge and tools all close to hand. Throughout the whole throwing process the hands and the clay must be kept well lubricated with water. This should be done with a scoop of the hand at any time you feel your hands beginning to bind on the clay.

With the wheel spinning fast anti-clockwise, fix the ball of clay firmly to the dry wheelhead by throwing it hard down as near the centre as you can. Wet the clay and place both hands round it with your thumbs crossed and resting on the top of the lump (fig. 21). Then push the hands very steadily together. This horizontal pressure from both sides will cause the clay to rise up into a cone. As it grows move the hands slowly up with it. Then push the clay down to the wheelhead again by the pressure of your right palm on the top of the cone while steadying the side with the fingers of your left hand (fig. 22). Moving the mass up and down in this way helps to finally temper the clay and brings to the surface, where they burst, any small air bubbles left in it. You must avoid trapping air and slurry inside the clay on the upward movement or folding the clay over into a mushroom shape on the downward one, otherwise you will have trouble later when opening out the clay. Two or three of these coning movements will be sufficient.

After the last downward movement you should find with a little practice that the mass is spinning close to the centre of the wheel, but it may need a little extra pressure of the hands to coax it into the dead centre. Do this by returning your hands to the position shown in fig. 21. Push inwards and downwards with the palm of the left hand and the fingers of the right and push down only with the crossed thumbs. During this final centring movement it will be a help if you rest both forearms on the edge of the tray for additional steadiness. Put all the pressure of your hands on the clay alone and not on the wheelhead as well where it only acts as a brake and makes kicking tiring. Fig. 21 shows this very clearly. All the slip on the wheelhead is quite

21 Centring

undisturbed by the hands. A circle clear of slip appearing on the wheelhead is a sure sign that you are dissipating your energy by pressing on the wheelhead as well as on the clay.

I know that for beginners learning to centre is a difficult and often frustrating introduction to throwing. There is no substitute for frequent practice, and centring must be mastered before proceeding to further stages of throwing. Opening the ball and pulling up the pot wall with uncentred clay results in uneven and eccentric pots which tear or collapse before they are completed.

You will find that centring is easier if you keep several important points in mind.

1. The wheel must always revolve quickly and steadily for centring – at least 130 r.p.m. and faster if you can make it. There is a great temptation when you are having difficulty to slow down the speed of the wheel in the mistaken belief that it will help. In fact the opposite is true. You gain greater control if the clay passes more quickly between your hands.

2. Pressure of the hands should always be applied and released smoothly and gradually. Coaxing the clay is the only sure and effective way of centring. Sudden applications of pressure only make matters worse.

3. Try to learn to centre without always having to steady your arms on the edge of the tray except in the final stages. Many books ignore this point

but always locking your forearms can easily become a habit which later inhibits the free arm movements essential for throwing taller and wider shapes. It is also a cause of tension and early fatigue.

Opening.   Once the clay is centred you can safely make a hole in the middle of it to change the solid mass into a spinning wall. There are many different ways of opening, and each person will settle on a method which suits him or her best. The important thing is to support the outside of the clay very firmly while the opening is being made, otherwise the clay will be pulled off the centre. If this occurs it cannot be remedied and the clay is better cut off and another attempt made.

The method I use for opening small and medium pots is shown in fig. 23. It is a very simple method involving no change in hands or arms from the final centring position. With the wheel spinning quickly as for centring gently feel for the middle of the clay with both thumbs and push them downwards, stopping about $\frac{1}{4}$ in short of the wheelhead. Then gradually move your thumbs horizontally away from the centre, keeping the fingers of both hands very steady against the outside of the emerging wall (fig. 24). This movement completed, raise both hands simultaneously to even out the wall from top to bottom. It will then be about $\frac{1}{2}$ in thick. To counteract the tendency of the clay to flare out at the rim this last movement should be slightly inwards as well as upwards, so that the wall tapers towards the

23   Pushing both thumbs into centred clay

rim. In figs. 23 and 24 the forearms rest on the edge of the tray for additional steadiness.

Finish the base before pulling up the wall of the pot. Place your right hand on the outside of the pot wall to support it and place your left hand inside the pot (fig. 25). Move the middle and third fingers of the inside hand steadily from the centre of the base to the edge, flattening it as you go. Firm pressure is necessary here. Many beginners' pots crack through

24 (*Top*) Opening the clay   25 (*Bottom*) Flattening the base

the base as they dry because the clay in the bottom has not been sufficiently compressed. Bases are also more satisfactorily flattened if the wheel is spinning quickly and the left hand movement is slow and steady, and not vice versa. See how in fig. 25 the thumb and index fingers of the left hand rest on the right for support. Keep both hands in contact with one another wherever you can throughout the whole throwing process, so that both act as one. You will have greater control over the clay in this way.

Beginners may have some difficulty gauging the thickness of the base. Accurate judgment will come with practice, but until you have some experience you can measure the thickness by pushing the point of the clay trimmer vertically through the centre of the base. The resulting pin hole is easily smoothed over with a touch of the finger. Bear in mind that some slight thickness of the base equivalent to the thickness of the wire will be lost when the pot is cut from the wheelhead.

Thinning the Wall. With the base finished and flat, change the position of the hands from that in fig. 25 to that in fig. 26. The left hand is held vertically inside the pot, the thumb resting on the back of the right hand. The right-hand index finger is crooked and held vertically, the other three fingers are clenched into the palm. Lift both forearms from the edge of the tray.

26 Thinning the
    wall

Squeeze the clay between the finger tips of the left inside hand and the knuckle of the right index finger. As the pot wall grows draw both hands up with it. The pressure should commence at the base of the wall and continue right to the rim. Keep both hands in contact with one another and never allow them to become dry. Sudden friction can pull the pot off centre or even tear the clay. If the hands are lubricated with sufficient water each upward movement will be continuous and flowing from base to rim. Don't try to thin the wall all in one go, but make several upward squeezing movements working each time from base to rim. Very steady and equal pressure from both hands is essential if the pot is to grow vertically. Be especially careful as you reach the rim. Ease the pressure at this point very gradually and take your hands from the clay gently. Slow the speed of the wheel slightly as you do so.

Finishing the Rim. If the clay has been well centred, all subsequent movements steady, and pressure evenly applied, the rim will be perfectly level. It should need very little attention beyond some slight compression. This is simply done by placing the middle finger and thumb of the left hand on the inside and outside of the rim and then pressing lightly on the top edge of it with the middle finger of the right hand. Some potters use a small piece of chamois leather for this operation, folding it lightly over the rim.

If the pot is only slightly off centre the rim can be levelled with a trimmer. Insert the point obliquely with, not against, the rotation of the clay and cut the wall as the pot spins through several revolutions (fig. 27). Steady the inside of the pot as you cut and then lift the surplus clear.

27　Trimming with a needle

The rim is a potter's final statement of a thrown form. Once some control has been gained over clay, rims should be given shape and emphasis by greater or lesser pressure of the inside or outside hand. A good strong rim makes a pot look completed and not merely abandoned as if the clay ran out at that point.

Sponging Out.   Before cutting off mop up with the sponge any water in the bottom of the pot and remove excess slip and slurry from inside and outside the pot wall. If you use a lot of water you ought to sponge out at the end of each stage of throwing. The amount of water needed for throwing will be learnt by experience. Some clays are certainly 'thirstier' to throw with than others and need more water. Ideally you should aim to use only the minimum to ensure adequate lubrication of the hands. Excess water causes the clay to tire. Throughout the throwing process the water you are heaping on the clay is gradually permeating between the tiny plate-like clay particles. If too much water gets between them they suddenly lose adhesion and the pot collapses as a result. The rims of pots, especially those of open shapes like plates and bowls, often split if the clay becomes tired.

Cutting Off.   This is a matter of confidence as much as skill. Remove surplus clay and slurry from the lower part of the outside wall with the wooden knife and then undercut the pot to make a grip for your fingertips (fig. 28). Take the wire, place it flat against the wheelhead on the far side of the pot and holding it as taut as you can draw it quickly towards you under the *revolving* pot (fig. 29). Remove any slurry from your fingers. Then place the tips of the first and second fingers of each hand under the bevel you made with the knife and lift the pot boldly and cleanly from the wheelhead and place it on a ware board (fig. 30).

This is the professional way of cutting off and it is well worth persisting with until you master it. It is so simple and swift that the wheel hardly

29 (*Top*) Wiring through   30 (*Bottom*) Lifting off

stops spinning. The thin pad of clay left adhering to the wheelhead makes an ideal surface on which to fix the next ball of clay.

The twisted wire also leaves an attractive whorl on the bottom of the pot which needs no further finishing. This method of cutting off can be used for any size or shape of pot which can be lifted from the wheel without distortion. Later, when the pot is leather hard, any finger marks or sharp edges can be smoothed with a finger or thumb.

Another method of cutting off is to undercut the pot as above then stop the wheel. Squeeze out a sponge to flood the wheelhead with water. Draw the wire under the pot. Some water will come with it. Slide the freed pot on the water to the edge of the wheelhead and then onto a batt or tile. If the pot refuses to slide pull more water under it until it is free. This method is, of course, much slower than the dry lifting one above and is really only for the fainter hearted. The base of each pot will need subsequent turning, and the wheelhead must be cleaned and dried before another pot can be made.

Cylindrical Forms. The above account describes the throwing of a cylindrical shape which can be used for many other upright forms not necessarily vertical when completed. Making cylinders is good throwing practice. Vertical pots require very even and equal pressure from both hands and once you can make a basic cylinder you will have the necessary control over clay to attempt many other shapes with confidence. Beginners should concentrate on getting their early pots an even thickness throughout. Successful thin pots will come with practice. From time to time cut a pot in half as in fig. 26. The section will give you a clear picture of your throwing, revealing those parts of the pot where you need to apply more or less pressure to achieve a uniform thickness.

Rounded Forms. Gently swelling forms are made from a cylinder by applying slightly more pressure with the inside left hand after the basic shape has been thrown. During the shaping the right hand should give good support to the outside of the clay wall, and the pushing outwards should be done gradually, working from base to rim each time. Forms that swell out and then move in are made by alternate greater pressure of first the inside and then the outside hand.

When shaping, the position of the hands in relation to each other is important. For outward movement the outside hand should be slightly lower than the inside one, and vice versa when shaping inwards. Many throwers feel that the inside hand is the positive emotional shaping force imparting vitality and spontaneity: the outside hand represents the intellect, restraining and correcting the form.

Forms which are so rounded that they approach a sphere are seldom satisfactory if pushed out from a basic cylinder. The wall becomes weak at its point of maximum tension and it collapses. Fuller rounded shapes should, therefore, be pushed outwards as the pot wall is pulled up and thinned, and only the final shaping left to the end.

For both gently swelling and more rounded forms the diameter at the rim must not be allowed to grow wider than that proposed for the finished pot. The top can always be widened if need be, but it is much more difficult to close in the clay. Some slight extra thickness ought also to be left at the base of the wall to support the outward weight of the pot and the fuller the form the more clay will have to be left. Any excess can be turned away at the leather-hard stage to achieve a wall of uniform thickness from top to bottom.

Collaring.   The very narrow necks of flasks and bottles are made by collaring the clay between both hands. It is almost impossible to close a wide pot to a very narrow neck so the diameter at the rim should be only just wide enough to allow the left hand to enter for shaping the form prior to collaring. Sufficient thickness of clay from which the neck can be made should also be left below the rim. Mop up any water in the pot before the neck becomes too narrow. A sponge held by a clothes peg at the end of a stick is a good tool for removing water from narrow-necked pots. It will often go in where the hand cannot.

Close the neck by placing both hands right round it (fig. 31). Push the clay gently inwards and upwards increasing the speed of the wheel as you do so. It is important to avoid downward pressure. Give the clay maximum

31 Collaring

support by keeping as much of your hands in contact with it as you can. Don't rush the process. Narrow the opening very gradually, otherwise the clay will buckle. Collaring causes the clay to thicken where it is compressed, so between each narrowing movement thin and pull up the neck by inserting one or two fingers of the left hand and applying gentle pressure with the right. The old Chinese potters used to impart additional tension to the form of narrow necked bottles by blowing gently into the new thrown pot.

Repetition Throwing. Any potter who enjoys throwing will want at one time or another to make a series or set of pots of a particular shape. For repetition work the balls of clay should be of similar or equal weight. The first pot can be measured with calipers or a ruler and subsequent pots made to the same size. For a quantity of a repeated shape it is worthwhile making a simple measuring gauge. You need only a thin pointed stick affixed to the edge of the tray by a piece of clay. If it is fixed into position so that the point almost touches the rim of the first pot, subsequent ones thrown to the point will be the same height and diameter as the original. Potters' suppliers also sell more sophisticated adjustable gauges which can be clamped to the side of the wheel. If, at a later stage, you wish to repeat a particular pot keep a record of the *wet* height and diameter, and the *weight* of clay needed.

Repetition throwing is rather out of favour these days. Many people mistakenly associate it with industrial mass production. They feel, fallaciously I think, that hand-made forms repeated in quantity automatically lack vitality and quality while the unique pot alone is, in some mysterious way, endowed with aesthetic significance. Yet no one who has practised repetition throwing and watched a repeated form change and develop over a period of time can doubt its importance in training a potter's skill and judgment. It gives an insight into form that can probably be gained in no other way, and also imparts to the throwing itself an easy rhythm which flows over into the making of all other thrown forms. Mindless repetition of undemanding shapes is undoubtedly stultifying, but repeating subtle shapes which constantly exercise both a potter's skill and imagination is of inestimable value in the struggle for real control over clay so that conceptions of form can more easily be given plastic reality.

Stack Throwing. This is a development of repetition throwing. It is quicker and more convenient to throw several small pieces from one large lump rather than trying to centre several tiny individual balls of clay. Small cups, lids, spouts and hollow handles are among the kinds of thing that can be thrown in this way.

A ball of clay weighing 3 or 4 lb is centred and pushed up into a cone or stack as in fig. 22. A small pot or lid is thrown from the top of the stack, cut off and further pots thrown until all the clay in the stack is exhausted (fig. 32). Estimating just the right amount of clay for each item is a matter of trial and error but fine judgment comes with experience especially if you practice making several items the same size. There is also little difficulty

in cutting each pot off level if the clay is first scored with the trimmer at the point where it is to be cut, and then cut off with a very short wire not more than 3 or 4 in long.

Throwing Larger Pots.   Large pots are difficult to lift directly off the wheel-head without serious distortion and they are, therefore, thrown on a batt. On completion both batt and pot are lifted together and the pot only removed from the batt when it is leather hard. Batts must be made of a durable and rigid material which will not warp. Asbestos batts, $\frac{1}{8}$ in thick, are excellent, especially if one side is smooth and the other slightly textured. Wooden batts should preferably be of marine or boil-proof plywood at least $\frac{1}{2}$ in thick. Potters' merchants sell batts but you can easily make your own if you have a bandsaw or know someone who will cut them for you. The most useful size batt for cylindrical and rounded shapes is 8–10 in, while 12–18 in will be necessary for wide dishes and flat plates.

Fix a batt firmly to the wheelhead as follows. Centre a ball of clay about 1 lb or so in weight, flatten it so that it is about $\frac{1}{2}$ in thick, and then score the surface (fig. 33). Slightly dampen the underside of the batt, place it on the pad of clay, centre it and then press it down firmly so that it is stuck securely. Turn the wheel to check that the batt is level, and adjust if necessary before commencing throwing.

The principles of centring and opening clay for larger forms are the same as for smaller ones, but the methods differ. The clay ought to be just a little on the soft side: centring large masses of stiff clay is very tiring work. Beat the prepared clay into an even shape and place it in the centre of the dampened batt. With a slowly revolving wheel beat the lump into the centre of the batt where it should assume a conical shape. The greater care you take over this initial beating the easier it will be to centre the clay.

With a large lump of clay the aim is to move off-centre clay from the point of greatest mass and resistance at the base to the point of least resistance and mass at the top.

Wet the clay, and with a fast wheel spin press inwards with both hands on the lowest point at the base. The mass will be too large to grow into a cone but it should assume a roughly conical shape. Rest both your forearms on the edge of the tray and lean your whole body weight against the clay. As the lower part becomes centred move your hands up the mass so that any unevenness is also moved up. When the whole of the lower section has been centred place your right hand on top of the lump and press downwards and inwards with it to centre the uneven clay on the upper part of the

33 Fixing a batt to the wheelhead

mass. At the same time keep the already centred lower part of the clay steady by firm pressure of the left hand. Continue to keep the left forearm on the edge of the tray for extra support and steadiness the whole time. The hand movements are really similar to those for smaller lumps of clay, except that the mass is centred in stages rather than all at once.

Open the clay by pushing in the centre with the whole palm of the right hand while steadying the outside of the mass by firm pressure of the left (fig. 34). Link the hands together throughout this action. Flatten the base as described above, but pull up the wall initially using the left-hand fingers inside and the whole of the right hand on the outside. Lock the hands together for steadiness. Take particular care and some time in opening out and during the early stages of pulling up the wall to prevent the clay from being pushed off centre. Slight irregularities which are of little consequence in a small pot can become so exaggerated in a large one as it grows that the clay gets completely out of control.

Once the wall is about $\frac{1}{2}$ in thick throughout, and only then, begin squeezing with the fingers to thin the wall. Keep the same thickness from base to rim all the time, and pull up slowly and gradually. Slow the speed of the wheel as the pot grows taller or wider. It takes more upwards movements to thin the wall of a large pot than a small one. At all times make sure that your arm movements are vertical or slightly away from your body. There is a tendency when pulling up tall forms for the hands to be drawn inwards towards the thrower. This strains the clay against the spin of the wheel at a very critical stage of the throwing instead of pulling it up gently with the spin. If the form grows very tall never try to push the clay up from below,

34 Opening clay for larger shapes

but get someone to kick or operate the wheel for you so that you can stand and continue pulling up the pot from above.

When the pot is finished sponge out, tidy the base of the wall, under-cut it slightly and wire it through so that as the pot dries it can shrink freely on the batt. Failure to wire through may result in the pot cracking through the base. Free the batt from the wheelhead by levering under it with a piece of wood. Do this at several places if necessary and be gentle, or you will lose the pot if the batt comes away suddenly. Lift batt and pot together and set aside to dry. When the pot is leather hard it can be easily and safely lifted off the batt.

Very wide open shapes tend to dry unevenly because the rim and wall are so much thinner than the base, and this happens however slowly the pot is dried. To overcome this, once the rim and wall are stiff enough to support it, place another batt across the rim. With one hand on each batt turn the pot smartly over and remove the batt on which the pot was thrown. The base will then dry faster and prevent serious unevenness developing.

Very Large Pots.   Particularly large pots can be made in stages by adding extra clay to the top or bottom of a previously thrown piece and continuing the form using the newly added clay. In this technique throwing and coiling are combined.

The initial pot should be thrown on a batt, not trimmed at the bottom but wired through and then restuck by pressing on the base with the fingers. Lift it from the wheel and dry this form very slowly to prevent the rim getting too dry. When the clay is firm but softer than leather hard, in fact as soon as you judge the pot wall to be capable of bearing the weight of new clay, return the batt to the wheel, re-centre it and fix it down. Score the pot rim, rub slip into the score marks and then place a thick, even coil of clay on the rim. Attach it carefully by fingering it down on the inside and outside of the original form. Pay particular attention to this joining and to the point where the two ends of the coil meet. Then revolve the wheel slowly and gently pinch the wall to make it even. This done, wet the clay, place the fingers and thumb of the left hand astride the rim and a finger of the right hand on its edge as it revolves. This movement will finally centre the coil. Thinning the wall upwards can then be done in the usual way. Steady the edge from time to time and trim off any slight unevenness if necessary. Finally tidy the base, wire through again and lift off.

Successive coils can be added in the same way and the pot made larger if desired so long as the wall is not thrown too thin to support the weight of extra clay. That part of the pot wall made from new clay will, being softer, shrink more than the rest of the pot. With experience you can judge what adjustments to make in the shape to compensate for this phenomenon. During the throwing you will only be able to shape the newly added clay: the stiffness of the initial form precludes any further shaping by throwing below the line where the new clay joins. If the whole shape needs to be altered it is best done by gentle beating when the pot is leather hard.

Chapter 4

Turning and Attachments

TURNING

Certain shapes which can be thrown only with an excess of clay in the base or lower part of the pot wall need to be shaved down or *turned* when the clay is leather hard. Open bowls, dishes, plates, some narrow-necked vessels and some kinds of lids are finished in this way.

Turning is obviously a far less sensitive way of forming clay than throwing. Stiff clay has nothing like the responsiveness of wet clay and no turning tool has the subtle touch of a finger. Moreover all the turning is done on the outside edge only. Consequently even very sensitive turning seldom, if ever, enlivens a thrown form and clumsy turning quickly deadens it. With certain shapes some turning is unavoidable, but from an aesthetic point of view it ought to be kept to a minimum.

Turning tools are made of metal, about 8 in long, $\frac{3}{4}$ in wide and about $\frac{1}{16}$ in thick. You can very easily make your own, or get them from suppliers. The ends are bent at right angles and the cutting edges ground to a chisel section. Bright mild steel tools are best. They have a reasonably hard-wearing cutting edge which can be easily sharpened with a file. It is useful to have several turning tools with cutting ends of various shapes (fig. 35).

Pots intended for turning must be dried as evenly as possible so that the clay responds well to the cutting tool. Only pots which are reasonably well centred are worth turning; the walls of an eccentric pot will already be of uneven section and any subsequent shaving will only exaggerate this weakness – leading perhaps to distortion or even cracking during drying and firing.

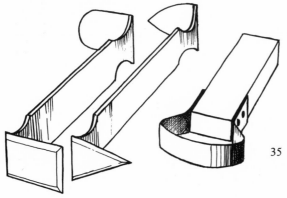

35   Turning tools. The one on the right is made from a short length of steel strip used to bind packing cases.

Turning ought to be done as soon as the pot is stiff enough to lift without it bending, though you must use your judgment here. Large pots will bend because of their size alone, even though the clay is stiff enough for turning. Ideally a pot ought to be at that leather-hard stage where the clay, when cut, comes away cleanly in long ribbons. If it is too soft the inner profile of the pot may easily be distorted by pressure of the turning tool, and if it is too hard the tool only polishes the clay instead of cutting it.

Pots that are no wider at the top than the wheelhead, and which have good strong rims for the pot to safely balance on, can be turned by simply inverting them on the wheel. They must be centred before being turned and this is best done by revolving the wheel slowly and gently tapping the pot with the left hand *against* the spin of the wheel. This is not quite as simple as it sounds and it does require practice, but once learnt it is the quickest and surest way of centring any shape. Another way to centre is by trial and error, checking by marking two concentric circles on the base. Once the space between the circles is equal all round the pot is centred.

Fix the pot down by means of three pieces of stiff clay at the rim, thumbing them well down on the wheelhead. Place the clay sufficiently close to the rim to anchor the pot securely but not so close that it distorts the rim shape in any way.

When the inverted pot is centred and secured kick the wheel fairly quickly and shave away the thicker clay until a good profile is obtained and the pot is of even thickness throughout (fig. 36). Judging the thickness of the wall and foot is largely a matter of experience, but some idea can be got by tapping the clay and gauging the thickness by the sound. As you cut keep

36 Turning. The hands are linked together for steadiness.

69

in mind the inside shape, so that the inside and outside form both retain the unity of the throwing. Hold the turning tool very firmly in the right hand and steady the base of the pot with the left, putting on just sufficient pressure to prevent the pot from flying off the wheel yet not so much that the wheel can't turn freely. As in throwing, keep both hands in contact with one another for greater steadiness.

Ease off the sharp cutting where the harder line of turning meets the softer finger ridges of throwing so that the transition between the two different surfaces is gradual and not abrupt.

Bowls thrown with a generous thickness in the base to allow for the cutting of a footring from which the shape can spring should have their profile turned first and the foot hollowed out after (fig. 37). Use a tool of

38 Simple clay chucks:
1 Narrow necked bottle held inside a chuck;
2 Wide bowl supported on a chuck;
3 Dish much wider than the wheel supported on clay attached to the rim of a jar which is in turn fixed to the wheelband.

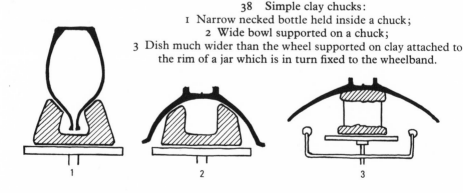

appropriate size and shape and cut the foot from the centre outwards allowing a margin of clay for further correction. Try to see that the inside shape of the foot continues the main lines of the pot. A too shallow foot looks mean, but a good generous one adds considerable interest to the shape of many open forms, the best of them combining grace with stability.

Pots which are wider than the wheelhead, or which have delicate rims or slender necks, are turned either in or over a chuck. This is simply a thick-walled pot a little drier than the leather-hard form it is to support (fig. 38).

Centre and secure the chuck as above and then shape its rim with a turning tool to fit the inside or outside profile of the pot it is going to support. Lightly dampen the rim, place the pot on or in the chuck and revolve the wheel to see if it needs some slight adjustment. Once the base is level when it revolves the pot is centred. Put a little pressure on the base to anchor the pot firmly to the chuck but don't overdo it. Clay sticks to clay with surprising tenacity at times. There is no limit to the diameter of pot that can be turned by this method so long as the chuck is tall enough to lift the rim of the pot clear of the tray.

The only technical fault likely to arise in turning is a phenomenon known as chattering. The clay suddenly develops a regular rippled surface which continued cutting only seems to exaggerate. Chattering is caused by a blunt tool, clay which is too hard, an unsteady hand or any combination of these things. It can be cured by temporarily changing to a turning tool with a triangular cutting end and gently shaving the clay with just the point of it until the surface of the pot is smooth again.

ATTACHMENTS

Attaching a handle to a pot or covering it with a lid almost invariably pre-supposes it is performing a useful task. And there is no doubt that handling and using an attractive thrown pot that also works well is a source of constant pleasure to the user. Just how well it functions depends as much on the care and attention given to the making and joining of any attachments as on the throwing of the pot itself.

Fitness for purpose, I think, ought to be the prime consideration with things like handles and spouts, but provided that they are considered and felt in relation to the pot itself and complement the form, nearly all attachments will enhance a pot aesthetically as well as functionally.

All attachments are joined as soon as the pot receiving them is leather hard. Any necessary turning is done before the attachment is added. Once the pot becomes too dry it is impossible to add an attachment to it without cracks developing at the joint because of the uneven shrinkage of the two parts, though some clays are more forgiving in this respect than others.

Unfortunately clay dries whether you are there or not, and it isn't always possible, if potting time is limited, to put on handles etc. at just the right moment. In this event pots can be kept damp in a tightly lidded polythene bin or in a cupboard lined with polythene sheeting with a slab of wet plaster in the bottom. In such conditions pots will remain damp for surprisingly long periods. Pots that are just a little dry can be softened by dunking them for a moment in water.

Lids. The simplest lids are those thrown all in one piece off a stack. Estimate the amount of clay required for the lid and isolate it at the top of the stack by collaring the clay to about half its diameter. Push both thumbs, a little way apart, down into the top of the stack to make a groove with a small mound of clay in the centre of it (fig. 39). From this mound the knob is shaped and the lid then extended outwards by the pressure of the index fingers of both hands until it fits the pot. Check the diameter with calipers. Then cut the lid free with a short wire and lift off (fig. 40).

39 (*Left*) Simple lid needing no turning thrown off a stack

40 (*Below*) Lifting off the lid

Lids thrown in this way, provided that they are accurate and carefully cut off, need no further finishing apart from wiping a thumb round the bottom edge where they were wired through. If necessary they can be trimmed for tidiness or a better fit by turning them, upside down, in a small chuck.

Lids of the kind above have no flange so they must be accommodated just below the rim of the pot in what is called a gallery. While the pot wall is being thinned leave a thickness of clay at the rim. Press the inner half of this gently downwards with the left thumb, nail pointing outwards. Use the index finger of your left hand to support the clay being displaced and to guide it inwards (fig. 41). Having thus formed the gallery compress the inside edge to prevent it chipping in use. For the same reason don't make the gallery thin and weak. Leave the final shaping and thinning of the pot wall until after the gallery has been formed.

Domed lids with a flange can either fit over the rim of a pot or rest in a gallery, whichever is most appropriate for a particular shape. Small lids of this kind can be stack thrown, but larger ones will need a separate ball of clay. In either case flanged lids are made in two stages. They are first thrown upside down and a knob added later, at the leather hard stage, after turning.

Throw a very shallow bowl with a generous thickness of clay at the rim. Press downward on the outer half of this thickness with the right thumb against the supporting middle finger and gently squeeze the clay outwards horizontally. Contain and compress the edge of the emerging flange with

73

42 Throwing a flanged lid upside down

the left-hand index finger (fig. 42). The amount of overhang on the lid
and the depth of the flange are determined partly by the amount of clay left
at the rim and partly by the form the lid is to cover. For simple covers the
flange need only be shallow and the overhang the same diameter or slightly
more than the pot. Lidded pots intended for pouring need lids with a deep
flange to keep them in place when the pot is tilted. Measure the diameter of
the lid with calipers. For a lid fitting over the rim you need only measure the
inside diameter of the pot, allowing $\frac{1}{16}$ in to $\frac{1}{4}$ in of free play between the
outside of the flange and the inside of the pot. For a small flanged lid seated
in a gallery – as in a teapot for instance – two measurements – the inside
and outside diameters of the gallery – must be considered for each lid.
Flanged teapot lids can be locked into their galleries for safer pouring
by pulling a tiny lip on the flange in the same way as for a jug.

When the lid is leather hard re-centre it right way up and turn the top
to the inside profile. Then score the centre and rub in a small amount of
thick slip. Take a small piece of soft clay, shape it to a ball and press it
firmly but gently onto the score marks. Don't overdo the pressure or you
will press right through the lid. Thumb down the edges of the ball. Wet
your fingers and with a fast wheel spin centre and shape it to form a knob
(fig. 43). If the lid is for a tea or coffee pot bore a hole in the lid before setting
it aside to dry.

Knobs can be turned out of a thickness of clay left in the base but they
are less satisfying. A thrown knob is the most comfortable to grasp having

been made for the fingers by the fingers. Moreover it seems to grow organically out of the lid, a feeling impossible to achieve by turning alone.

There are some limits, however, to the size of thrown knobs. Because of their solid thickness very large ones run a risk of cracking in the biscuit firing. This can be overcome by cutting a plug of clay out of the knob from inside the lid to make it less solid, by throwing a hollow knob, almost like a small pot, or by fixing a loop of clay across the top of the lid as a handle.

Handles.   For thrown pots the most appropriate handles are those pulled out from a lump of clay. This method allows the size and shape of each handle to be considered and most closely related to the form of each individual pot.

Use clay the same consistency as for throwing. Some books advise using stiffer clay but this, I think, is a mistake. It offers greater control while pulling, but only at the expense of vitality. Stiff clay is too unresponsive for good lively handles.

Take a well-kneaded lump about 2 lb in weight, beat it into the shape of a large carrot, and then hold it outstretched in your left hand at shoulder height. Wet your right hand and begin pulling out the lower part of the clay (fig. 44). The section will be round or oval at first but, as the clay grows, pull it so that the section is flat. Keep the pots in view while you pull the handles to give fullest consideration to their width and section. The back of the handle may be left plain or, by adjusting the position of your fingers,

75

44 (*Left*) Pulling a handle

45 (*Below*) Attaching the handle, top joint

it can be simply and very effectively decorated by forming various ridges and grooves appropriate to the pot shape.

When you judge that the lower part of the handle is about the right width and thickness lay it on a clean ware board and cut it off smartly with a sharp downward movement of the right thumb against the edge of the board. Pinch the tail end of each handle so that they are all the same length. Leave all the pulled handles to stiffen for about a half hour.

Score the pots and rub in a little thick slip. It is only necessary to score the top point of attachment. Take a handle close to the butt end between your right-hand thumb and index finger. Now slightly thicken and shape this end by tapping with your left-hand index finger. The angle at which you do this will determine the direction in which the handle springs from the pot. Put your left hand in the pot to support the wall behind the joint. Then holding the handle back a little from the butt end still between the right thumb and finger push it firmly into the score marks without squeezing the clay in any way (fig. 45). As you push support the tail of the handle with the little finger of the right hand. Seal the joint without distorting the handle.

Now hold the pot in your left hand at arm's length so that the handle is pointing vertically down. Wet your right hand and pull the handle out a little further to smooth out any irregularities and to adjust the final width and thickness (fig. 46). Then loop the handle over into an appropriate curve,

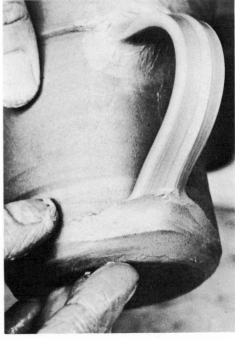

(*Left*) Smoothing out any irregularities   47   (*Right*) Spreading the bottom joint to ensure a sound fixing

supporting it if necessary with a finger or two of the left hand. Fix the bottom of the handle very lightly, check that it is straight, and then smartly cut off any surplus with a sharp downward movement of the right thumb at right angles across the width. Finally spread the bottom joint into a fish tail shape using two quick movements of a wet thumb or finger, pressing from the centre of the handle to first one side and then the other at an angle of 45 degrees. This both makes a decorative feature of the join and ensures that a large area of clay at the bottom of the handle is securely fixed to the pot (fig. 47).

The function and appearance of handles are closely related. Many good pots are too easily spoilt by handles which seem clumsy or ungenerous or which fail to work well. A handle should be easy and comfortable to grasp and provide good control for pouring and lifting. Wide handles with a flat section give the best grip and are also lightest in weight and appearance. Handles that loop close to the pot give greater control than those which curve unnecessarily wide. The most satisfactory curve is nearly always the one which takes the minimum number of fingers necessary to lift a particular size and weight of pot.

Every shape of pot has a different centre of gravity. Consequently the places from where a handle springs and rejoins a pot also determine the degree of control for lifting and pouring. Positioning a handle so that it works best calls for fine judgment. Some handles work and look best if they spring from the rim, others from the wall of the pot.

Apart from a necessary and inevitable thickening at the top joint, the appearance of all handles is improved if the edges are kept parallel from top to bottom. Handles which taper sharply to the bottom always look weak and mean.

Straight Handles. Handles suitable for small bowls or jugs may be attached at one end only so that they protrude straight out and up from the side of the pot. They are first pulled as above but into a preliminary shape slightly thicker and shorter than required. The butt end is attached to the pot, the handle pulled out to the appropriate length and width and the end then pinched off. A good thickness of clay should be left at the butt end to make a strong joint and give the handle a generous appearance. If necessary the pot can be inverted until the handle is stiff enough to keep its shape unsupported.

This kind of handle is limited to about $2\frac{1}{2}$ in to 3 in in length. Larger handles attached at one end only are hollow. They are thrown from a stack, cut off with a trimmer, and later attached to the pot at a suitable angle when leather hard, in the same way as for spouts.

Lugs. These are robust ears of clay usually attached to the opposite sides of cooking and oven pots to facilitate lifting. They ought to be sufficiently generous in size to be easily grasped through a thick cloth when hot. Lugs are made in exactly the same way as handles, but are attached to the pot along their whole length. They should be pulled with a roughly triangular section, cut off in equal lengths and left on a board to stiffen slightly.

To attach them first score the whole surface which is to receive the lug and rub in thick slip. Take an end of the lug in each hand and bend it to the curve appropriate for the pot – tall pots need an almost semicircular curve, shallow pots a very gentle one. Flatten one edge of the curve by gently tapping it on the board. Place this edge against the score marks and finger the top side of the joint well down. The underside can be safely left. Secure both ends of the lug by smoothing them down onto the wall of the pot. Finally run over the top of the joint with a wet finger and then ease up the outer edge so that the lug points outwards.

Lips. The shaping of pouring lips for jugs and pitchers is done by taking advantage of the plastic nature of clay immediately the pot has been thrown prior to cutting off. The first two fingers of one hand support the outside of the rim while the clay between them is gently extended outwards into a lip by a slight rocking movement of the first finger of the other hand (fig. 48). There are no infallible rules concerning the pouring properties of lips but I have found that one of generous sized width with parallel sides and not too much overhang generally pours well without dripping and also looks attractive.

48 Pulling a lip on a jug

It is essential that clay used for jugs is highly plastic and well matured and the throwing rapidly completed before the clay gets tired. Short or tired clay will split because of the strain in pulling the lip. The throwing itself must be very even with no weakness in the upper part of the wall or the pot itself will distort as the lip is pulled out.

Spouts. These are made initially in the form of small slender pots tapering throughout their length from a wide base. They may be thrown off a stack but I think a greater variety of shape can be obtained by using a separate ball of clay each time. Before making spouts place the pots receiving them near the wheel to help you gauge the most appropriate shape and size.

Begin by centring a small lump of clay with a broad base. There is no need for a spout to have a bottom so press right through to the wheelhead when opening out. As you thin the wall give it a sharp and continuous even taper from base to tip by alternately pulling up and collaring. A fast wheel spin is essential here because of the small diameter of the spout. Use the left-hand index finger inside to begin thinning the wall, and then use the little finger as the aperture narrows. Make the wall as thin as possible because a thick spout always looks clumsy. It is better to throw the spout too long than too short as any excess clay can be trimmed off at the joining stage. When the spout is finished make a deep undercut at the base, wire through, lift off and set aside to stiffen until it is leather hard.

To join the spout place it against the pot and roughly gauge its position. Then pare away excess clay at the base with a thin sharp knife until it fits the profile of the pot exactly when held at the right angle. Here the length of the spout is important. The lower tip of it should be level with or slightly above the gallery otherwise it will be impossible to fill the pot without liquid pouring from the spout. Next place the spout in position against the pot and lightly trace the outline of its base with a sharp point. Set the spout aside and within the line you have drawn, allowing for a thickness of clay at the base of the spout, make holes for a strainer. Strainer holes should be kept close together and there ought to be as many as the space will allow if the pot is to pour well. A piece of sharpened hollow tube about $\frac{1}{4}$ in in diameter is the best tool for the job. By gently twisting it through the walls of the pot it cleanly removes a plug of clay where a solid pointed instrument would only compress and displace it. Any ragged clay edges on the inside of the pot created by the passage of the hole cutter should be left until the pot is dry when they can be easily smoothed over with a wooden tool or wire loop. For coffee pots there is no need for a strainer and one large hole may be cut instead.

Next score the area around the strainer and rub in thick slip. Take the spout and checking that it is at right angles to the pot, press it firmly on, thumb down the base and smooth it over with a wet finger. Because of the nature of plastic clay nearly all thrown spouts tend to twist clockwise in the firing. Set the spout, therefore, in a position slightly anti-clockwise to that required in the finished fired pot. Once the spout is in place trim and

49   Attaching a teapot spout

smooth the tip of it. A sharp lower edge helps to prevent dribbling by
cutting cleanly the flow of liquid, but it is vulnerable to chipping and some
compromise will have to be struck between functional efficiency and
durability.

A tea or coffee pot is perhaps the most demanding yet fascinating to make
of all thrown pots. First the pot has to work well; it has to be stable and
well-balanced, be comfortable to hold in the hand and pour well. These
desirable functional attributes can be achieved mainly by sound technique,
by good throwing and by careful and considerate assembly. But secondly
the pot has got to look and feel right, and this means making all the parts
not in isolation but with the others in mind, so that when the pot is assembled
it will possess a strong unity of form. To achieve this requires feeling and
imagination, and technique plays only a minor role.

In many ways tea and coffee pots epitomise the perpetual and intriguing
task that a potter faces in making any kind of pot with an attachment: that
of reconciling the demands of function with his own ideas of what is beautiful
and good.

Chapter 5

The Decoration of Raw Clay

The urge to decorate clay has always been very strong. Neolithic man scratched patterns on his simple pots and while there have been times in the past when pottery forms were simple, even austere, there has never been a period when they were totally devoid of decoration. Surprisingly simple and unlikely clay objects have been embellished. Set into the ridge tiles of my own workshop, once the village blacksmith's, are several tiny chimneys which ventilated the forges. Each chimney is covered by an inverted clay bowl, no more than six or seven inches across, wheel thrown by hand towards the end of the last century. There is nothing very remarkable about them except that round each cover runs a single line of a Greek key pattern impressed in the soft clay by the thrower. The decoration can only have been done for his own delight: from the ground twenty feet below it is invisible.

So far in this book I have described how a very tangible raw material can be transformed methodically stage by stage into pots of various kinds. The subjective nature of decoration defies this approach. The raw materials for it are abstract and elusive. The techniques and tools used can be described, but the kind of marks they make and where on a pot to put them are so much more spontaneous acts of the imagination than gestures of the hand that it is impossible to lay down fixed rules.

The most fruitful approach to decoration is, I think, to start at the end rather than at the beginning, to look first at decorated pots wherever you can find them in workshops, books or museums and see what attributes they possess. Then keep these in mind when you come to decorate pots yourself.

What I think you will find in a well decorated pot are qualities something like these. First, the potter has respected the surface character of the pot and the decoration is in keeping with it. Delicate brushwork or fine incising on a small flawless porcelain piece, for example, would be inappropriate on vigorously thrown, large earthenware pots. Secondly, the decoration is in scale with the pot, the marks are the right size for it, neither dominatingly large nor timidly small. Thirdly it has variety, whether it is a contrast of line or texture or different sizes of brushmarks. In this context asymmetry is nearly always more varied and interesting than symmetry. Fourthly, the decoration has a feeling of unity about it: however complex it appears the design holds together as a whole and is closely related to the form of the pot. Fifthly, it is executed with conviction, vigorously and spontaneously. Lastly, it has freshness and vitality. This can take many forms: it may be simplicity, a startlingly apposite image, a fresh touch or some new way of using a familiar tool or old technique.

Ideas for decoration come ultimately from the subconscious mind but they can be triggered off by natural forms, by the patterns of leaves and branches, by the textures of stones, wood or by the shapes of birds, fish and animals. Many found natural objects like fossils, shells and worn pebbles are a fruitful source of ideas. Tools also are a great source of inspiration and it is worthwhile collecting any kind of object that will make attractive marks in or on clay – such as pieces of wood both blunt and pointed, old broken hacksaw blades, nuts and bolts, combs, wire loops, pieces of string and brushes of all shapes and sizes. The discovery that certain marks can be made with a particular tool can often stimulate a whole new range of decorative ideas. Lastly, and most important, look at pots of all kinds and periods. They are a perpetual source of ideas, not only for decoration but for shapes as well. I am often surprised at the numbers of people who start pottery as a hobby at home, or go to pottery classes, or even become professional potters and yet work in isolation, cutting themselves off from this unlimited supply of imaginative information just a little of which would greatly help to improve their skill and increase their pleasure in making pots by hand.

As you decorate try to keep in mind some conception of the finished form, because whatever is done to the surface of a pot in its raw state will later be affected by glazing and firing. Some decorating techniques exploit the plastic nature of clay by cutting or impressing the surface so that a glaze will pool in the hollows or break thinly over any high spots. Others take advantage of the interaction between slips, glazes and fire to produce surfaces of great variety and richness. Several techniques can be combined provided they don't destroy the scale of the pot. Generally speaking the smaller the pot the fewer techniques you can employ on it.

DECORATING WET CLAY
Although almost all raw clay is decorated when leather hard the surfaces of freshly thrown pots can be enlivened before they leave the wheel. The wet clay may be cut or incised with any kind of wood or metal tool. Very gentle pressure will only mark the surface, while greater pressure (and some care) will alter the shape of the pot without making it structurally weak. The main form can be squashed or squeezed, necks and rims can be made oval or have pieces pinched out of them to add interest and variety.

OTHER FORMS OF DECORATION
Beating. As a way of radically altering shapes this technique is confined mainly to thrown pots. When the pot has stiffened but before it is leather hard it may be beaten with a flat piece of wood into geometric or asymmetric shapes. The beating should proceed gradually working systematically round the pot. Where a sharp angle is required beat the pot first and then

scrape two adjacent sides with a metal or rubber kidney. Interesting forms can arise by creating a contrast between an angular base and a circular rim.

Impressed Decoration.   Impressing small objects into clay to make decorative patterns must be done at just the right stage of drying. The clay should be soft enough to yield to the impress but not so soft that it readily distorts the pot shape. If the clay is too dry the image will be indefinite. Always support with one hand behind that part of the pot wall which is being impressed, otherwise the clay may split. You can achieve subtle variety within the pattern itself by impressing to varying depths or by contrasting smooth and impressed surfaces. To avoid distortion, impressed decoration on tiles, slab-built pots and pressed dishes should be done on the rolled-out clay before any cutting to shape or moulding is done.

Impressed patterns can be left to fill with glaze or they may be emphasised by brushing over with oxide or slip. A loaded brush will flood the hollows while an almost dry one will just catch the high points. Some particularly lovely textures can be made like this.

Another way of emphasising impressed pattern is to fill them with a contrasting slip, a method known as encaustic or burnt-in decoration. Large bold patterns work best. Many very beautiful mediaeval tiles for English churches and monasteries were made like this. A non-plastic material such as flint or very fine grog should be added to the thick slip used for filling the impressions to prevent uneven shrinkage. When both slip and clay have dried to the same state the whole surface can be pared down until it is level and the inlaid pattern sharp and clear.

Roller seals can be used to make a running repeat pattern around a pot. The chimney covers referred to at the beginning of the chapter were decorated in this way. The roller is simply made by scratching a bold pattern around a small solid cylinder of leather-hard clay through which a hole is then bored. After the roller has been biscuit fired, a wire handle is attached to it and the pattern applied by holding the roller against a soft pot as it revolves on the wheel.

Incised decoration.   Leather-hard clay lends itself to a wide variety of techniques which involve cutting into the surface. Fine lines can be engraved in the clay with a sharp tool. A slight chisel edge is more responsive than a point and wooden tools more sensitive than metal ones. Any burrs thrown up by the cutting should be left until the pot is dry when they can easily be removed.

The stoneware teapot made by the author (colour plate 8) was decorated by incising into the clay. The parallel lines were applied using a wooden tool immediately after throwing and the vertical cuts made with a wire loop-ended tool at the leather-hard stage. The semi-matt grey green glaze has broken over the high spots to emphasise the pattern.

Pots can be fluted by cutting away the top surface of the clay. Wire loop-ended tools are best for this. Potters merchants sell them in various shapes and sizes but excellent home-made ones can easily be fashioned from the steel strip used to bond packing cases. Depending on the size of tool fluting may be very delicate or vigorous and bold. The surface of a pot may also be cut into very definite facets by shaving away up to half the thickness of the wall with a sharp knife or metal kidney. Thrown pots treated in this way should be purposely left thicker as they are being made.

By cutting away the area of clay surrounding a pattern relief decoration is possible. One must take care not to overdo this as very bold relief can create an uneasy three-dimensional effect on the surface of the pot.

Holes may be cut right through the wall of pots with only a decorative function to create pattern. The thinness and delicacy of small pieces, particularly porcelain, are emphasised by this kind of perforation.

Applied Decoration. As well as being cut away clay can be added to a pot in the form of ropes, strips or thin slabs for decorative effect. These additions should be joined as soon as the clay is stiff enough to handle. They may be impressed or incised before they are joined, or the joining itself can be given decorative emphasis by vigorous thumbing and twisting. Clay applied in this way is a particularly organic and generous form of decoration, growing freely out of the nature of plastic clay. It is at its best on pots of generous size and robust shape (see colour plate 2). Many English mediaeval jugs and pitchers were splendidly embellished in this way.

Clay Seals. These combine applied and impressed decoration. A small mould is made first by cutting or modelling a motif into the end of a solid cylinder of clay which is biscuit fired. This is then used to impress the motif into a small pad of soft clay attached to the leather-hard pot. Pigment or slip can be brushed into the hollows made by the mould or the powdered glaze wiped off the high spots to emphasise the seal (fig. 50).

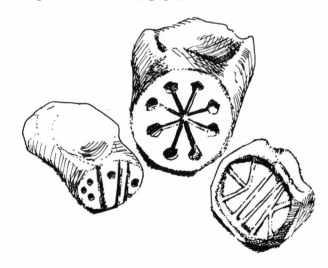

50   Biscuit-fired clay seals

SLIP DECORATION

Coating a pot with a layer of slip, or engobe, as it is sometimes called, opens up a very wide range of decorative possibilities. Slip is a creamy mixture of clay and water, with sometimes a small percentage of colouring oxide added. It is applied by dipping or pouring, usually when the pot is leather hard. It will affect and itself be affected by the colour and degree of transparency of the glaze which subsequently covers it. In fact one of the great attractions of slip decoration is that the interaction of slip and glaze often results in surfaces which are richer and more varied than those obtained from glazes alone.

Slip must adhere closely to the clay body during both drying and firing. Any cracking of the slip coating or flaking on rims and edges is a sign that the pot and slip are contracting at different rates. It follows, therefore, that the most satisfactory slip is usually one which contains as much as possible of the clay used to make the pot itself.

To make a slip which is darker than the clay body it is sufficient to add a small amount of colouring oxide to it. Any slight adjustment to ensure good fit can be made by adding a small proportion of a more plastic ball clay or a less plastic china clay.

Very pale slips, however, are more difficult. A white slip made entirely with china clay will flake off because of its relative low contraction rate, but a satisfactory compromise may be possible using a mixture of china clay and the body clay or a pale plastic ball clay. But if the resulting slip is still not white enough or does not fit the clay well the only recourse is to biscuit fire the pot and then cover it with a slip which has a low contraction rate. In this event it will prove advantageous for satisfactory adhesion of the slip and for the glaze fit if you incorporate in the slip mixture about 15–20% of both flint and a leadless frit for earthenware, and the same quantities of flint and feldspar for stoneware.

The high clay content of slip somewhat restricts the colour range to more earthy shades. Bright clear colours are better achieved from glazes alone although greater colour intensity may be had by glazing over a pale or white slip, especially if the clay body is dark.

One ought to regard the use of slips as a means of achieving subtle colours with a variety of surface texture. Perhaps the most interesting effects are those obtained from semi-opaque glazes which only partially and subtly reveal the slip beneath.

Colouring Slips. Slips are coloured in exactly the same way as glazes (see chapter 9) by the addition of small quantities of metal oxides or carbonates.

The list opposite gives some suggested percentages and an indication of the resulting colour.

% by dry weight	Colouring agent	Resulting colour
$\frac{1}{2}$–2	Cobalt oxide or carbonate	pale blue to dark blue
1–5	Copper oxide or carbonate	pale green to dark green
2–6	Iron oxide	light to dark brown
4–10	Manganese dioxide or carbonate	light to dark purple-brown
1 3 8	Cobalt oxide Manganese dioxide } Iron oxide	variegated blue-black

Preparing slips. Weigh a required amount of body clay and place it in a bucket with the appropriate amount of colouring oxide. Add clean water and pass the mixture through an 80-mesh sieve into a second clean container. Using plenty of water will make sieving quicker and easier and prevent the clay from reuniting into lumps after it has passed through the mesh. Leave the slip to settle and then decant surplus water until it is the consistency of thick cream. Only mix large quantities of slip after you are satisfied by testing that the recipe fits your clay.

Application. Apply slip by dipping or pouring. Pots to be slipped should be leather hard and any attachments allowed to become quite stiff, otherwise they may sag out of shape as they absorb water from the slip. Certain parts of the pot, bases and galleries for instance, can be kept clear of slip by painting them with wax. This resist technique is more fully described below.

Leather-hard pots are fragile, but slipping them is not hazardous or difficult if you remember:

1. To work quickly so that the pot has no chance to absorb excessive water which might lead it to soften and perhaps collapse.

2. To grasp the pot only where it can safely take the strain of your fingers – never on rims or edges.

Before you begin, stir the slip well and make sure that it is free from lumps. Slip that has been standing for any length of time may need to be re-sieved before use.

If both the inside and outside of the pot are to be slipped do the inside first. Pour slip into the pot, swill it round, then quickly pour out the surplus. It is not necessary to fill the pot to the rim provided the pot is twisted as the slip is being poured out. Wipe off any drips on the outside with a damp sponge. Leave the pot to dry a little before doing the outside. Do this by spreading the fingers of one hand inside the pot to give a firm grip. Then plunge the pot bottom-down into the slip up to the level of the rim. As you lift it out support the base with the other hand and gently shake off any surplus.

Where only part of the outside needs to be done the pot may be grasped by the foot and immersed upside down in the slip stopping short of the fingers. Air pressure will prevent slip entering the inside more than just a little way. Care must be taken that the rim of the pot is level with the surface of the slip before being immersed and that it remains vertical during the operation. A second dipping to correct an unsightly slanting line may result in the pot absorbing so much water that it collapses.

Where the size of the pot makes dipping the outside of it impracticable slip may be poured on. Support the pot upside down across a bucket by means of two sticks, preferably of triangular section. Pour slip on the pot, moving round it as you do so. Use a jug of generous capacity so that pouring is continuous. It is essential to remove the bowl from the sticks as soon as possible because some slip will adhere to them and gradually eat into the rim causing it to disintegrate. Triangular sticks minimise this tendency but do not eliminate it.

Slip Trailing. While the pot is still wet from dipping lively patterns may be drawn on the damp surface using a slip trailer filled with slip of a contrasting colour. The simplest kind of trailer is a rubber bulb fitted with a pointed nozzle.

Slip used for trailing must be very well mixed and sieved, and thicker than for dipping. Glazes have a dissolving effect and slip which is too thin tends to disappear in the firing. Adding a small quantity of gum arabic or tragacanth will make the slip more viscous and help it to adhere more closely to vertical surfaces.

The point of the nozzle should almost but not quite touch the surface of the pot, and it ought to be drawn backwards trailing the pattern behind it. Press the bulb gently and steadily to ensure a clean and even line of slip. The speed at which you move the trailer determines the width of line and its thickness. Direct the movements generously from the shoulder and not just from the wrist. If necessary hold the trailer in both hands for greater control.

Speed and confidence play a major part in slip trailing. Once the pattern is begun there is no time for pause or hesitation. It is essentially a swiftly executed and lively technique, and patterns should, therefore, be simple and bold. To gain confidence practise first before trying it on your pot. If you use waxed or greaseproof paper for this much of the slip can be reclaimed.

Feathering. This form of decoration was traditionally used for press-moulded earthenware dishes. Roll out a slab of clay on a piece of hessian and place them both on a board. Pour the background slip into the centre of the slab, swill it round to cover all the clay and drain the surplus back into the bucket. Hold the clay against the hessian while you do this.

While the slip is still wet trail close parallel lines of a contrasting colour

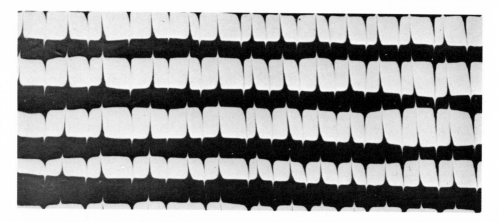

across it and then lightly bump the board on the bench. This sharpens the edges of the trailed lines and flattens them.

Now draw the tip of a feather or a single stiff broom bristle across the lines at right angles. One slip will be drawn delicately into the other. Some lovely patterns can be made by drawing the feather at right angles first in one direction and then in another (fig. 51). Traditional harvest motifs were trailed in a similar way using lines and dots of slip which were drawn out with a feather into the shapes of wheat and barley ears. Once the slip has lost its shine and is no longer tacky (but before the clay stiffens too much) the slab may be placed over a hump mould and then trimmed.

On thrown pots the lines are usually trailed like spokes radiating from the centre outwards, and the feathering drawn parallel to the rim.

Marbling. On the freshly slipped inside surface of a dish or on a slab of clay prepared as above, pools and dots of a contrasting slip can be blobbed at random. The pot or slab is then violently shaken and twisted, causing the slips to run into each other to produce the appearance of marble (fig. 52).

51   (*Top*) Feathered slip decoration   52   (*Bottom*) Marbling

Obviously chance plays a major role in this technique and it isn't always successful. It can, however, reprieve from the slop bin a pot which has been unsuccessfully trailed!

Combing. Patterns may be combed through coatings of wet slip using a comb made of wood, leather or stiff rubber. The teeth need to be rounded and spaced not less than a quarter of an inch apart. The comb is dragged at an oblique angle over and through the slip as soon as it begins to lose its shine. The displaced slip subtly reveals the contrasting clay body beneath. Combing can be done freehand or with a gentle up-and-down movement against a pot slowly revolving on the wheel.

Sgraffito. Once a coating of slip has dried a little, patterns may be cut clearly through it to reveal the clay body, a technique known as sgraffito. The freshness and vitality of this kind of decoration is greatly affected by the condition of the clay. If it is too dry it is far less responsive to the cutting tool. Ideally the clay ought to be a little on the soft side and the pattern cut as soon as the coating of slip has dulled. A chisel ended point makes the most sensitive drawn line; large areas can be cut away with a wire-loop modelling tool. Leave the removal of any burrs until the pot is dry (colour plate 4).

Resist Decoration. Contrasts between slip and body clay can also be effected by coating selected parts of the pot with wax. When the pot is dipped the slip will not adhere to the waxed surface. Patterns may be drawn or painted with a brush or trailed using an expendable empty plastic washing-up liquid bottle. Potters' suppliers sell proprietory resist medium but it is far cheaper and just as good to use a mixture of hot melted candle wax and kerosene (paraffin).

Exercise caution in preparing the resist mixture. Never directly heat the wax and kerosene in a pan by themselves. The mixture may easily overheat and catch fire. The safe way is to place a bowl containing pieces of chopped candle and a small quantity of kerosene in a pan of water. The heat of the boiling water will be sufficient to melt the wax without danger providing reasonable watch is kept.

When hot the wax should flow freely from the brush. If it seems too stiff remove the pan from the stove, add a little more kerosene to thin it to the right consistency and re-heat. The edges of the pattern will vary in character, either sharp and crisp or soft and blurred, depending on the thickness of the wax. In the biscuit firing the wax will burn away.

Cut paper patterns can be similarly used for resist decorations. Thin brown paper is good for this. It must be pressed closely onto the surface to prevent slip seeping behind and blurring the edges. Lightly damping the pot helps to ensure close adhesion. After dipping the paper can be removed as soon as the slip becomes dull. The leaves of plants can be used in exactly the same way (see colour plates 9 and 10).

Slip Brushing.   Slip applied by loaded brush has a more varied surface than one attained by dipping, but only really bold and thick brushings are satisfactory. Fine brushwork painted with slip is seldom successful because the actual colouring oxide is such a small percentage of the mix that it tends to disappear in the glaze firing. Brushes used for slip must be large and full, capable of taking up a good quantity of liquid. They need to be recharged at frequent intervals during the painting to ensure a sufficient thickness of slip. Far Eastern potters used coarse brushings of white slip called 'Hakeme' which provided a pale but variegated background for contrasting brushwork applied later after biscuit firing (colour plate 3).

Chapter 6

Drying Clay and Biscuit Firing

When clay is fired we cannot actually see the tremendous chemical changes taking place in the kiln. Therefore before passing on to glazing and firing it is, I think, important to understand what happens to our soft, plastic, permeable raw material on its journey of transformation into a dense hard and permanent substance.

DRYING AND FIRING CLAY

This process begins from the moment your completed pot is put aside to dry and await the kiln. All plastic clays contain a high percentage of water. Most of it is added by the potter to make the clay soft and workable and this may constitute as much as 25% of the whole. But some water is also not just mixed with the clay but is actually a part of its integral molecular structure. This is water which chemically combined with the clay during the millions of years of weathering and it is present even in clay which seems absolutely dry.

The water we add ourselves surrounds each tiny clay particle with a film of moisture. As this slowly evaporates from the drying pot the clay first stiffens and then hardens. The clay particles close to occupy the space taken up by the water and as a result the pot shrinks. The more plastic the clay and the finer the particles the greater the shrinkage. Some plastic clays may shrink as much as 10% from wet to dry.

All clays also gradually become paler as they dry, and once this change of colour is complete and uniform throughout the pot is dry enough for the kiln. It must be stressed that clay is never absolutely dry, only as dry as the air surrounding it, and in a high humidity atmosphere the moisture content may, therefore, still be quite high.

The dryness of large or thick pots can be deceptive. They may appear pale and dry on their outer surfaces but still be quite damp inside. To be sure they are dry right through they ought to be put in an airing cupboard or somewhere quite warm for at least 24 hours and taken from there straight to the kiln. If they are removed from a dry warm place and left standing they will reabsorb moisture from the atmosphere and return to a damper state: they become what potters call 'shop rotten'. Some potters test for dryness by putting a pot to their lips – when dry the pot is no longer cold to the touch.

The final drying of clay actually takes place in the early stages of firing.

As the temperature of the kiln passes boiling point (100°C – 212°F) any residual water is driven off as steam. This water may only be a very tiny amount, as little as 1% or less, but as it turns to steam it expands in volume enormously and very suddenly. If it cannot escape quickly enough through the pores of the clay it will crack or even burst the pot in order to get out. It is, therefore, very important that the early part of the firing is sufficiently slow and gradual to allow moisture to escape. The larger and thicker the pots the slower the early part of the firing must be.

At about 350°C (662°F) chemically combined water begins to be driven off and by 600°C (1112°F) the process is complete. This dehydration is an irreversible chemical change and once it has taken place the clay, though still friable, is in fact now pottery. It has lost all its plasticity and will no longer slake down in water.

All clays contain quartz and at 573°C (1065°F) the quartz particles change from one kind to another, from alpha to beta quartz. This quartz inversion, as it is called, causes the clay to expand slightly in volume by about 2%. On cooling the same thing happens in reverse and the clay contracts again to its original size. Heating and cooling should not be too rapid, therefore, at this critical temperature.

Most clays also contain a proportion of carbonaceous matter, which darkens their colour, and other impurities such as sulphur. With heating these burn away, which is why biscuit-fired pottery is always lighter in colour than the raw clay. It is important to burn out all this carbon: if some remains in the clay it can cause glazes to become discoloured and, in severe cases, even cause blisters in the clay and glaze, a phenomenon known as bloating. It requires time as well as temperature to burn off carbon matter, and too rapid a firing may leave some still in the pores of the clay. Generally speaking carbon is burnt off by 950°C (1742°F), although some clays may need temperatures in excess of 1050°C (1922°F).

With advancing heat clay hardens and tightens until it becomes hard, dense and impervious, the point known as vitrification. Clays vary enormously in the speed and temperature at which they vitrify. Red clays containing a high percentage of iron may vitrify at 1000°C or even less, while china clays will still be soft and porous at this temperature and will not be vitreous until 1500° or 1600°C (2732° or 2912°F). Vitrification is always accompanied by shrinkage.

If the temperature of the kiln goes beyond the point of vitrification pots begin slump out of shape and deform. Hotter still and the clay itself begins to melt into a liquid which on cooling becomes a glass.

Potters obviously stop short of these temperatures, except in the case of porcelain, where the clay is fused sufficiently for it to almost glassify. It is this fusion which gives to porcelain its hardness and translucency. It can also contribute to the high failure rate of porcelain pots, for any over-firing beyond the point of fusion causes the pots to deform as the clay itself begins to melt. Successful firing of clay consists of heating it to the temperature at

93

which it is hard, dense and tough enough to serve the purpose of the particular kinds of pottery which you make.

BISCUIT FIRING

Glazed pottery is usually fired twice. There is a preliminary biscuit or bisque firing followed by a hotter glaze or glost firing. Glazing necessitates considerable handling of pots, and as clay in its dry raw state is very fragile the risks of glazing raw pots are considerable.

The biscuit firing imparts a degree of mechanical strength to the clay and renders it sufficiently robust for glazing. Also it enables decorative and glazing techniques to be employed that are very difficult or impossible on raw clay. The temperature of the biscuit firing will vary from clay to clay. Too low a temperature and the pots will not have sufficient strength to withstand the strain of their own cooling; too high and the pots will be so dense that they lack the degree of absorbancy necessary for successful glazing. Clay manufacturers will recommend suitable biscuit firing temperatures for individual clays, but as a general rule biscuit temperatures are not critical: about 1000°C (1832°F) will be found satisfactory for most clays.

Setting the Biscuit Kiln. Set about biscuit firing in an orderly manner. Sort out the dry pots into groups of a similar size and shape and put them on a table or shelf close to the kiln. You will find that having rather more pots than the kiln will hold gives you a wider choice for more economical kiln setting. As the pots are unglazed there is no danger of them fusing together and they can be stacked in the kiln one on top of another or placed inside one another. The only things to avoid are putting too heavy a load on pots at the base of stacks, and wedging pots so tightly inside one another that the outer one is unable to shrink freely against the inner one. With experience a potter learns to fill the kiln with great ingenuity, fitting a surprising number of pots into quite small spaces.

Regular and similar shapes and sizes will need few kiln shelves if any, and the setting space can be filled with pots alone. Mugs and jugs can be placed rim to rim, base to base alternately. Lidded pots stack similarly, one right way up, one upside down, from kiln floor to arch, with their lids in place but inverted. Bowls are demanding of setting space. Smaller ones can be fired inside larger ones. Similar sized ones can be set rim to rim with a smaller pot between, or stacked inside one another. If the fit is too tight place a small quantity of grog in each bowl so that when stacked the rims are not quite touching. This is the most economical method of biscuit firing quantities of bowls. Prop all stacks against one another to prevent them from falling over (fig. 53).

Irregular shapes must be placed on kiln shelves, each one supported by three props (see page 108). This is the minimum number required and also the most stable. Where successive levels of shelves are built up the props must be directly over the ones below. In this way the weight of both shelves and pots rests directly on the floor of the kiln and not on part of individual

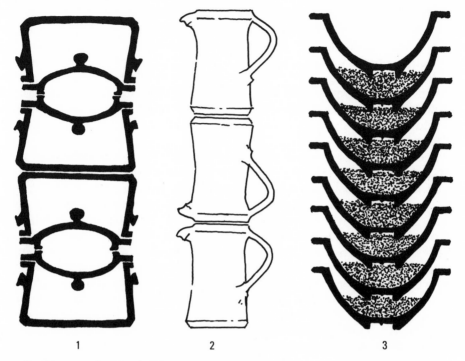

53 Stacking pots for biscuit firing:
   1 Lidded pots stacked rim to rim with lids inverted;
   2 Jugs stacked base to base, rim to rim;
   3 Bowls stacked with a small amount of grog in the bottom of each to prevent rims touching.

shelves. Careful attention to this point will prevent the early fatigue of shelves.

Very heavy objects should be supported by additional props, any necessary levelling of shelves being done by placing pieces of grogged clay on top of props. On no account should shelves rest directly on top of pots. In electric kilns pots should not touch the elements and in flame-fired kilns remember to leave a passage between the pots for the gases to pass.

A biscuit firing is not affected by slight overfiring and one cone bending at about 1000°C (1832°F) (cone 06 or 05) will be sufficient. It should be set, slightly tilted, in a small wad of well-grogged clay and placed where it can be clearly seen through a spy hole. Make sure that when it bends it will not touch any pot. (The use of pyrometric cones for judging kiln temperature is fully described on p. 109.) Close the kiln door or brick-up, as the case may be, but leave the sealing of cracks in brick doors until the firing is well under way.

Firing the Biscuit Kiln. The early stages of biscuit firing must be slow to avoid cracking the ware. A rate of 50°–60°C (120°–140°F) per hour will be fast enough for the first two or three hours. Electric kilns should be on a low thermostat setting; gas and oil burners should be turned as low as possible. In wood fired kilns a small fire should be lit from very thin sticks burning on the ash pit floor at the very front of the firemouth. A fire that will burn on the firebars proper will probably be too fierce at this stage. With all fuel kilns it will be an advantage to pre-heat the chimney in some way before lighting the kiln. A small fire of sticks or a propane gas torch inserted in the base of the chimney will warm it sufficiently to start a gentle draught moving through the kiln. Without this, combustion may be difficult in the early stages of the firing.

Once the kiln has reached about 150°C (300°F) residual water will have been driven off. The burners can then be turned up a bit, or more wood added little by little until the rate is increased to about 80°–100°C (175°–210°F) rise per hour. This rate can be steadily maintained until the cone bends. If you haven't a pyrometer you can determine when evaporation is complete by holding a mirror or cold metal rod close to an open spy hole. If little or no condensation takes place on the mirror or rod it is safe to slowly increase the heat. Now is also the time to seal off any cracks between the brickwork in the door with a mixture made up of equal parts clay and sand.

Biscuit firings should be as oxydising as possible so that all carbon and other impurities are burnt away. With electric kilns this will be automatic. With oil and gas burners you should make sure that there is sufficient primary air (air which is mixed with oil or gas in the burner before combustion) to the burners to ensure complete combustion.

The chimney damper should also be open sufficiently for a slight pull of secondary air (air that enters elsewhere, through the burner ports or through special holes under the firebox) to pass through the kiln. The amount of secondary air shouldn't be too great, otherwise it will cool the flame and the temperature will not rise. Constant oxydation is difficult with wood fired kilns. Each new baiting with wood tends to create smoke and consequently reducing conditions. But the kiln atmosphere will be predominantly oxydising if wood is added a little and often, rather than infrequently in large quantities. As the temperature advances it will be possible and necessary to transfer the fire from the ashpit floor to the firebars.

When the kiln is cherry red regularly check the cone every ten minutes or so. Low temperature cones soften and bend rapidly. Once the cone has fallen right over maintain a soaking heat, during which the temperature does not vary, for about half an hour. The biscuit firing is now completed.

The heat should then be turned off or, in the case of wood-fired kilns, the fire left to burn through until it reduces to embers. The pots must be protected from cold draughts during cooling, or they may dunt (crack). All burner ports, fireboxes and ashpits should, therefore, be sealed off with pieces of kiln shelf or tile, and any cracks clammed tight with the clay/sand mixture. Next, dampers should be pushed right in to close off the chimney to prevent any cold air from being pulled into the kiln. Finally, any cracks which have appeared in the door bricks should be clammed tight and spyholes sealed.

The heat will escape slowly and gradually through the walls of the kiln and it will cool within a couple of day to 100°C, at which temperature it is safe to open it. Do this gradually by opening the door little by little, or by removing a few bricks at a time.

Biscuit Faults. As you unload the kiln check each pot for possible faults and flaws. Sound pots will ring true when tapped, cracked pots have a dull, hollow note. Below are the most common biscuit faults with their causes and remedies.

1. *Pots burst or shattered*
CAUSE: The pots were too damp or there was too rapid a temperature rise at the beginning of the firing for the thickness of the pots or both.
REMEDY: A slower increase of heat up to 150°C (302°F) and particular care around 100°C (212°F) when residual water is driven off.

2. *Cracks running in from rims*
CAUSE: This kind of crack is usually, though not invariably, a sign of dunting. Cold air has struck the pots at a critical stage of cooling.
REMEDY: More thorough sealing of all cracks through which cold air can be drawn into the kiln. Check that the damper was pushed in completely.

3. *Hair-line cracks, especially round the base of larger pots*
CAUSE: Usually an indication that the pots have not reached a temperature high enough for them to withstand the strain of their own cooling.
REMEDY: Fire a cone higher or soak at the top temperature for a longer period or both.

4. *Cracks where handles, knobs etc., join*
CAUSE: This is primarily a fault at the time of making. The pots were too dry when the attachment was added and uneven shrinkage has caused the joint to open.
REMEDY: Press a very stiff mixture of waterglass and clay into the crack and cover it with an extra touch of glaze. Better still, of course, join handles etc. before the body of the pot becomes too dry.

5. *Pots cracked diametrically across and through the base*
CAUSE: This may happen either because the base was too thick and escaping steam has caused the crack, or because the clay in the base did not receive the same amount of compression as the walls of the pot. This is more likely to be the case only with a thrown pot.
REMEDY: Make the base thinner, or compress the clay more when forming the base (see chapter 3, page 56).

6. *Rims chipped or split*
CAUSE: Rims were not strong enough to withstand the weight and strain of pots above.

97

REMEDY: Place larger pots with stronger rims at base of stacks; build shorter stacks; or place pots on shelves.

7. *Small pieces blown off outer surfaces of pots*

CAUSE: Usually a result of some foreign body in the clay, particularly stones or plaster.

REMEDY: Fill with stiff waterglass/clay mixture as above (4) and cover with glaze; remove clay with more care from plaster drying slabs. Some impurities you will have to live with.

8. *Pots flashed or toasted on one side*

CAUSE: The passage of flame and heat has struck the pots more on one side than the other. In cases of large pots this local heating may cause the pot to crack because of uneven shrinkage as the clay heats and cools. This is especially the case with very wide plates and bowls.

REMEDY: Build the bag wall (see page 118) higher to protect pots from flame impingement; or pack pots more openly to allow a better passage for heat and gases.

9. *Discolouration of ware*

CAUSE: This is usually because of uneven heating or carbon remaining in the clay due to reduction or low temperature, or both.

REMEDY: Refire at higher temperature in oxydising atmosphere. In actual fact this will be necessary only where discolouration is severe. If it is mild it seldom has any ill-effects and can be safely ignored.

Chapter 7

Kilns

There can be no pottery without great heat, and the management of fire is an essential and particularly exciting part of making pots. In fact it is no exaggeration to say that fire is central to a potter's work. It preoccupies him at every stage. It partly determines his choice of clay; and the care he takes over making his pots has much to do with ensuring their safe passage through the fire. Many potters – and I would count myself among them – regard their kiln with an ambivalent feeling; it produces their greatest triumphs, and it contrives at their darkest failures.

THE DEVELOPMENT OF KILNS

Simple kilns were in use at least 10,000 years ago and the changes that have taken place in kiln design and construction have been, until comparatively recently, the result of endless experiments, of trials and errors. This empirical approach must inevitably have meant the enormous forfeit of much fine creative work, and one can only marvel at the patience and perseverence of potters throughout the ages in the face of such losses. It is only within the last 150 years or so, with the growth of industrial ceramics, that systematic research has been conducted into the technology underlying kiln design, construction and firing. Even so, kilns remain essentially very simple pieces of equipment. Despite the uncertainty, perhaps even mystery, which surrounds the firing process, few kilns are too complex to operate or to build even for those with little experience.

The earliest potters dug shallow pits in the ground in which they placed grasses, twigs and branches for fuel. They piled the pots on top, placed more fuel in and around them and covered the heap with more grasses and twigs and pieces of broken pots. The fire was lit and more fuel added until the pots glowed red-hot. Wet grasses and stalks were then put over the pots to retain the heat and within the short space of an hour or two the firing was completed. To withstand the shock of sudden heating and cooling very open sandy clays were used and the pots pre-heated before firing. Even so the failures were considerable and a high percentage were lost. These pit firings are still done today by many potters throughout the world, particularly in parts of Africa and South America.

Though such firings are quick and need no kiln structure as we know it, the heat generated is too low to make hard, durable pottery, and to melt glazes. Nevertheless, whatever their technical shortcomings, the aesthetic qualities of countless pots fired in this way are very impressive.

The history of kiln development is a fascinating one and readers who wish to pursue it more fully are recommended to read *Kilns: Design, Construction & Operation*, by Daniel Rhodes (Chilton Book Co., Philadelphia, 1968). Basically it is the story of potters finding ways to raise the maximum temperature at which their wares are fired by improving fuel combustion and conserving the heat thus generated.

It was discovered for instance, that pit firings were more successful if air holes were constructed in the base of the pit. The fuel burnt better because more oxygen was present to help combustion. A wall built round and over the pots in the pit retained more of the heat generated and also acted as a chimney, drawing more air into the fire and improving combustion still further.

From this it was a short step to the building of *up-draught kilns*, in which the heat from a firebox enters the setting space from below, passes up through the pots and exits at the top of the kiln. As might be expected such kilns fired unevenly; pots closer to the firebox were subjected to greater heat, and much useful heat was lost by upward convection. Nevertheless this type of kiln remained the basis of all firing in Europe from the time of the ancient Egyptians until the beginning of the nineteenth century (fig. 54).

54   Simple up-draught kiln

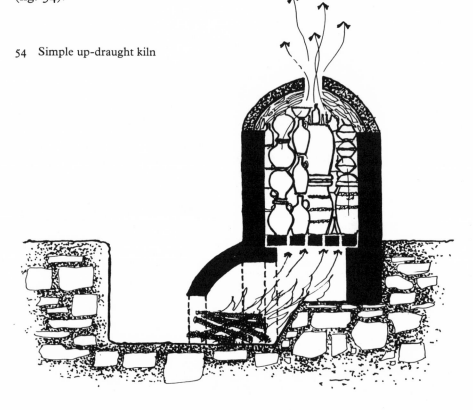

The most interesting and ingenious kiln developments came out of China and Japan. There potters discovered that by forcing the heat to exit at the same level as it entered the kiln much greater heat conservation was possible and the temperature throughout was more even. This type of kiln, known as *down-draught*, was certainly in use by 1000 B.C., and temperatures were achieved in them not reached in Europe for at least another 2,500 years.

By joining several down-draught kilns together, using the natural slope of a hillside to induce the draught, Japanese and Chinese potters were able to construct kilns of enormous capacity – capable of holding upwards of 100,000 pots (fig. 55). Such kilns were fired with wood and the escaping heat from one chamber pre-heated the next with great economy of fuel. As one chamber reached its maturing temperature the stokers passed to the next and so on until the whole firing was completed. Whole communities of potters would share a kiln, stoking day and night for perhaps a week or two. The pots from such kilns, particularly during the T'ang and Sung Dynasties (A.D. 618–906 and A.D. 960–1279) represent some of the finest achievements of ceramic art. Aesthetically and technically they remain unsurpassed, and have been for many modern potters a perennial source of inspiration.

55   Oriental down-draught climbing kiln

Kilns today are available in many sizes and fired by a variety of fuels. They can be purchased ready-made from kiln manufacturers and potter's merchants or you can build a kiln yourself. The size, temperature range and fuel used will greatly determine the kind of pottery you can make. The characteristics, advantages and drawbacks of various fuels for kilns are described below. But before finally making up your mind it is well worthwhile consulting other potters, seeing their kilns at first hand, and hearing how their kilns work in practice.

All kilns work on the same principle. At their most basic they consist simply of a chamber in which the pots are set, and the release of heat energy causes that chamber and its load to be heated to a required temperature. Kilns burning carbonaceous or hydrocarbon fuels such as wood, gas or oil require, in addition to a setting chamber, a firebox in which to burn the fuel and a flue or chimney to let the gases generated by combustion escape into the atmosphere. Electric kilns work entirely by radiant heat generated by electrical resistance. As a result they need neither firebox nor chimney.

Oxydization and Reduction. With the exception of electricity, all the fuels mentioned above release heat by the reaction of carbon in the fuel and oxygen in the atmosphere. Such fuels offer potters a choice of different atmospheric conditions within the kiln during the firing cycle. If sufficient oxygen is allowed to enter the firebox at all times combustion of the fuel is complete and the resulting firing is said to be *oxydising*. If, however, during certain parts of the firing cycle the amount of air entering the firebox or combustion chamber is restricted, incomplete combustion occurs and carbon monoxide gas or free carbon, in the form of black smoke, enters the kiln. At high temperatures carbon is avid for oxygen and combines freely with it wherever it can be found. In our case carbon seeks out oxygen among the metal oxides, particularly iron, in both the clay and the glazes, and combines freely with it. The metal oxides give up their oxygen and are thereby reduced to either their approximate or basic metal states. Such a firing is said to be *reducing*. In practice reduction firings are almost entirely confined to stoneware. They will be described more fully in Chapter 10.

The differences between oxydised and reduction fired pottery is quite marked; clay and glaze effects and surfaces obtained by one cannot be reproduced by the other. The radiant heat of electricity is always oxydising and electric kilns do not, generally speaking, offer the choice of atmosphere obtaining from other fuels. This can be a crucial factor in deciding which kind of kiln to buy or to build.

Some potters do attempt reduction in electric kilns by pushing charcoal, wood or even moth balls through the spy hole to induce smoke but reduction is seldom even and there is considerable risk of damaging the heating elements. However, a recent development whereby the elements are encased in protecting silicon carbide rods may offer a solution to one of the problems of electric reduction firings.

Electric Kilns. These are a fairly recent innovation made possible by the development and use of insulating refractory bricks which are light in weight and easily cut to shape. Since World War Two they have grown enormously in popularity and almost every secondary high school now has at least one.

They are manufactured in a great variety of sizes from 1–40 cu. ft. and are, without doubt, the most convenient of all kilns. The heat is produced by metal elements which run in grooves cut into the walls and floor of the kiln. All the elements are graded to ensure even heating and, provided their maximum service temperature is not exceeded, the life of elements is considerable. For kilns firing up to 1100°C (2012°F) elements made from an alloy of nickel and chrome are used. Kilns for higher temperatures up to 1350°C (2460°F) have Kanthal elements. This is a patented alloy manufactured by the Kanthal Corporation of Bethel, Connecticut, and these elements are very widely distributed and fitted in most high-temperature electric kilns throughout the English-speaking world. The heat input is regulated by means of switches or thermostats.

As all the heat is radiant no flue or chimney is needed and the kiln will, therefore, fit in almost anywhere. They are usually encased in metal, have taper-fit locking doors and, provided they are correctly installed, are very safe. They are also virtually silent in operation – a point your neighbours will appreciate! Little skill or experience is needed to operate them and indeed they can be fully and automatically programmed to both switch themselves on and off at the right time and temperature. Firings are also very uniform: there are none of the very variable results which often emanate from carbon-fuel kilns. Small and medium sized ones are also portable so that if you move house you can take it with you without dismantling it. Small kilns will plug into an ordinary domestic power socket, though larger ones will need a special power supply installed. Models are available for either front or top loading, depending on the space you have available.

Electric kilns are, however, the most expensive to fire. This may not be an important consideration if the pots you make are small and you can pack a lot into the kiln. But for makers of larger pots the size of electric kilns may prove restricting. As all of the heat is by radiation and conduction electric kilns do not function well if they are large because the elements will just not heat the setting space. Few electric kilns, therefore, exceed 30 in across. Some manufacturers overcome this difficulty in heating by making large kilns which are very tall, but any large electric kiln is very expensive to buy, install and fire.

Their greatest limitation, however, concerns the kind of pots that electric kilns produce. No genuine hand potter aspires to the bland uniformity of industrial wares and the often predictable results of electric kilns deny many potters the excitement of the unforeseen and the unexpected. Some of the most appealing qualities of glaze surface and clay texture result from a living flame licking in and around the pots. This is especially true of high-fired ware and potters making stoneware and porcelain often find electric kilns limiting.

Gas Kilns. These are available commercially in a variety of sizes from about 3 cu. ft. upwards in both up- and down-draught designs. Unless you build your own they are more expensive to buy but cheaper to fire than electric kilns. They are also less portable, and most gas kilns will almost certainly need to be dismantled if moved. With slightly different burners they can be adapted to fire town (coal), natural or liquid petroleum gas (L.P.G.).

Gas enters the firebox or combustion chamber through burners where primary air is mixed with it. The proportions of gas/air mixture can be precisely controlled and oxydising or reducing atmospheres easily obtained. Some provision is also made, usually by means of a small opening under the firebox, to draw in secondary air so that the heat will pass more easily through into the setting space.

Some kinds of gas burner are noisier than others, but generally speaking gas kilns are fairly quiet. The only sound is that of combustion. If you already have a mains gas supply to your house or workshop the installation or building of a gas-fired kiln should present few difficulties. The only two serious considerations are the siting of the kiln, because of the need for a chimney, and the nature of the gas supply itself.

Obviously there must at all times be sufficient gas reaching the burners to achieve your maximum temperature. This supply is governed mainly by the size of the gas meter but also by the diameter of the supply pipes and the distance of the meter from the kiln. Your local gas company will be pleased to help you on these points and it is a good idea to consult them at each stage. They will also be able to advise you about any local building, planning or safety regulations. Firing with natural gas is cheaper than with electricity.

Liquid petroleum gas is a by-product of the petroleum industry and a general term for butane and propane gases. It offers an alternative method of gas firing if a mains supply is not available. Its only disadvantage over natural gas is the higher cost per firing and the need for generous storage. Quite a large tank is needed to store L.P.G. even for a small kiln. If space is restricted several small tanks can be linked to a manifold and L.P.G. drawn from them all simultaneously.

Companies selling L.P.G. will be glad to advise on its use and sell or rent storage tanks. L.P.G. has, however, one dangerous characteristic. It is heavier than air and can, therefore, escape unnoticed from leaking equipment. If it collects in any quantity there is risk of an explosion. The best safeguard is a regular check of equipment by the L.P.G. supply company.

Oil- and Wood-fired Kilns. The kilns which follow are very much do-it-yourself affairs. The demand for oil- and wood-fired kilns from schools, colleges and potters has never been large enough to stimulate their commercial manufacture. They are less convenient than the kilns mentioned so far for many reasons, but my own feeling is that the more exciting and unpredictable results originating from their use more than compensates for the extra trouble involved. Components for these kilns are very readily available, and the construction of any kiln is far from the daunting experience that many potters and would-be potters imagine it to be. How to set about designing and building a kiln yourself is described in the next chapter.

OIL-FIRED KILNS. Oil is at its best for medium and larger kilns from about 8 cu. ft. upwards. For sizes below this it is difficult to purchase burners with a sufficiently low and stable flame in the early stages of biscuit firing when the danger of cracking pots from sudden heat shock is greatest. Kerosene (paraffin) or gas oil (No. 2 diesel) are the best grades of fuel to use.

Basically there are two choices if you opt for oil firing – *drip feed* or *forced draught*. The former is largely self-explanatory. The oil drips onto a grid or channel at the mouth of the firebox and all the air needed for combustion is pulled in by the chimney. The burner equipment needed is, therefore, cheap and extremely simple. You could make most of it yourself with very little trouble. Drip feeding has one chief drawback. Until the chimney is hot and pulling strongly combustion of the oil may be poor, with resulting smoke.

Burners similar to those for gas kilns are used for forced-draught oil firing. A fan or compressor supplies the air for combustion and this mixes with the oil at or in the burner to break down the fuel into very fine particles which more easily burn on emission from the burner nozzle. In some types of burner only part of the air supply atomises the fuel in this way. The rest aids combustion in the firebox and is also used to regulate the length of flame at any particular temperature by imparting varying degrees of swirl to the flame pattern.

The results from oil are very good and at the time of writing it is probably the cheapest fuel. Kiln atmospheres can be easily regulated if required, and rapid rises in temperature are possible, enabling quite large kilns to be fired quickly.

These kilns do, however, need oil storage tanks which can take up space, and forced-draught burners are noisy. There is always a roar of combustion and a whine from the fan or compressor. In confined premises this could be very wearing, especially if firings are frequent. As with drip feed it is an advantage to be in an isolated position or to have understanding neighbours. New burner equipment is also expensive and for a small kiln hardly worth the outlay, but for larger kilns it may be well worth thinking about. Second-hand oil burners are sometimes available and costs can be saved in this way. Even taking into account the cost of burners and bricks an oil-fired kiln may cost less than a manufactured electric or gas kiln of similar capacity.

WOOD-FIRED KILNS. The labour involved in wood firing is considerable. Quite large quantities are needed even for small kilns and it must all be cut, split and absolutely dry before it can be burnt. Pots may have to be set in saggers (refractory boxes – the word itself being probably a corruption of 'safeguard') to protect them from direct flame impingement. This is very time-consuming and limits the number of pieces you can fire at any one time. The life of saggers is also short and they will need replacement. Wood firings are smoky, take comparatively longer than other fuels and stoking must be continuous. There is no opportunity to leave the kiln during the entire duration of the firing, and the state of the wood and the weather can play havoc with firing schedules – sometimes protracting them for hours longer than usual.

A formidable list of disadvantages! Yet many potters, even those who, like myself, use other fuels, regard wood-fired kilns as the only real ones and aspire to wood firing one day. All the greatest pots of the past were wood fired. The long, soft flame which results from the burning of dry resinous woods brings out the finest qualities of clays and glazes. The fortuitous and subtle changes of colour and texture on the shoulders of jars and bottles and on the horizontal surfaces of dishes caused by flying ash and licking flames are some of the most appealing qualities of hand-made pottery. If only for them the rigours of wood firing would be well worth the effort.

The heat output of various woods differs enormously. Some hardwoods have a high calorific value, but generally resinous softwoods with an open grain, such as pine, fir and spruce, make the best fuel for kilns. They release heat at a much faster rate than hardwoods and, more importantly, they burn with a long, soft flame.

Wood must be burnt in a large firebox so that a sufficient volume can be burnt at any one time to generate the heat required. Plenty of air must also be able to reach the fire for good combustion to take place. In fact an excess of draught to ensure a strong and steady pull of air through the kiln is essential if it is to work well.

To ensure good combustion wood can be burnt on a grate made from cast pig-iron firebars or from clay refractory enough to withstand the heat. For infrequent firings this latter arrangement will probably suffice. The ash drops through the grate into an ash pit below and accumulations may be raked out from time to time to prevent the draught from becoming choked. If firings are frequent the best method is to stoke the fire from above by burning logs of wood with their ends resting on two hobs. This kind of firebox is well described by Michael Cardew in his book *Pioneer Pottery* (Longman 1969). It is important with wood-fired kilns to build the inlet and exit flues of generous area to cope adequately with sudden bursts of gases as a result of intermittant stoking. Wood firing invariably produces smoke and the kiln should be sited so that it does not disturb neighbours.

KILN FURNITURE

There is one area of pottery making where the individual craft potter owes a particular debt of gratitude to industrial ceramics. The growth of a vigorous pottery industry over the last 150 years or so has also meant outstanding progress in the development of refractories, without which the potter's task would be far more difficult and uncertain. We have cause to be grateful for a wide range of high-temperature bricks for kiln building and for modern kiln furniture, especially kiln shelves and props.

The early potters had to be content with placing their pots on the beaten earth floor of the kiln or piling them one on top of another. So long as the ware was unglazed and unvitrified these arrangements worked well enough. But the discovery of glazes brought new problems. Pots that touch each other when glazes melt fuse together and remain stuck when the glazes cool. They have to be broken apart and always bear the scars and blemishes from the contact with one another. Ingeniously, oriental potters often left unglazed those parts which touched on shapes like bowls which stacked one inside another. You can see examples of these in many museums.

Saggers and Shelves. An improvement in kiln setting – the placing of pots in the kiln for firing – came with the use of saggers, refractory clay boxes or cylinders which contained the pots for firing and which protected them from direct flames and flying ash. The saggers were each separated by a wad of clay and then built up into stacks or 'bungs'. The chief drawback, of course, was that the saggers themselves took up much valuable space and limited the number of pots that could be fired at any one time.

Saggers are almost obsolete today and most potters fire their pots on flat refractory clay shelves supported by props made from similar materials. The shelves and props can be easily removed from the kiln and by using various sizes of each very flexible kiln settings are possible.

Shelves are manufactured in a very wide range of sizes and thicknesses to suit almost every conceivable kiln. They are made either from clays high in alumina or from silicon carbide. High alumina shelves are suitable for most potters. Provided that they are thick enough they will withstand 1300°C (2372°F) without undue warping and should, with care, give long service – up to perhaps 100 firings or even more. For temperatures up to 1200°C (2192°F) $\frac{1}{2}$ in will be thick enough for small and medium sized shelves up to 12 in square. For higher temperatures up to 1300°C (2372°F) with reducing atmospheres and for larger sizes you will need shelves $\frac{3}{4}$ in, 1 in or even $1\frac{1}{2}$ in thick, depending on the load. There is obviously greater risk of shelves bending at higher temperatures, and if very heavy pieces are placed on shelves too thin to bear their weight. The small extra cost of purchasing thicker shelves may, therefore, turn out to be an economy. Silicon carbide shelves are super-refractory, have better heat-conducting properties and a longer life, but they are very costly and probably only a sound investment for the professional potter.

The number of shelves required for a kiln will depend on its size and the shapes of pots you make. It's better to have too many than too few. You never know when you may want to fire a kiln filled with flat shallow dishes which need more shelves than tall jugs and bottles. When purchasing shelves for kilns fired with wood, gas, or oil remember that there must be a *vertical* passage between the shelves for the flames and gases to pass. It will, therefore, probably be necessary to use more than a single shelf to cover the whole shelf area. Kilns larger than 12 in square shelf area will need two shelves per level and bigger kilns four or more. For example, a kiln 24 in square inside will need four shelves per level, each shelf being $10\frac{1}{2}$ in × 11 in. When the kiln is full there will be, in effect, four separate stacks of shelves with a 2–3 in vertical gap between them. Shelves in electric kilns can directly abut one another on one edge, but a minimum space of $\frac{3}{4}$ in must be left between the other edge and the elements.

Props, Stilts, Spurs and Bars. The props on which shelves are built up come in a wide variety of shapes, sizes and thicknesses. Hollow tubular props are the most widely available and give very good service. They can be increased in height by adding extension pieces, short solid props with a protuberance at one end which fits securely into the end of a prop. Collars can also be fitted at either end of props to give greater stability and a larger area of support for the shelf above. Props of about $1\frac{1}{2}$ in diameter give good stable support up to about 8 in high, but above this 3 in diameter props are better. Each kiln shelf will require three props, and having a range of sizes will help you to fill your kiln closely and economically. Small rectangular props can be used on any face, each prop, therefore, giving a choice of three different heights (fig. 56).

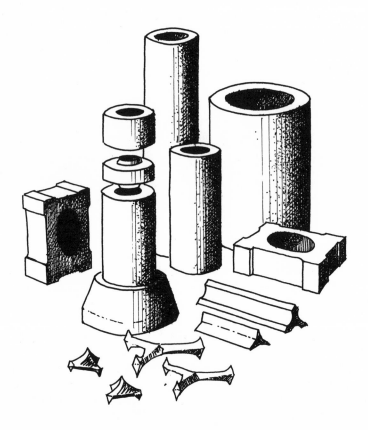

56   Kiln furniture: Props, extension pieces, spurs, stilts and bars.

Other aids to kiln setting are stilts, spurs and bars. Stilts are refractory pieces with three arms, with upward and downward points at the end of each arm. They are necessary for supporting pots glazed on the underside. Only the sharp points touch the glaze surface, leaving a hardly noticeable scar which is easily ground smooth. You can see these tiny blemishes under any industrially made plate or saucer. Bars are alternative supports to stilts and spurs. All these are only suitable for earthenware. The vitrification of stoneware at high temperatures causes pots to slump out of shape unless they are fully supported by a kiln shelf. Stoneware is unglazed on the underside for this reason. Special supports called 'cranks' for supporting tiles are also readily available. They enable many small flat objects to be fired in a limited space.

TEMPERATURE INDICATION

You can, like the early potters, judge the temperature of your kiln by eye alone, but this does require great experience. More certain temperature indicators are *pyrometric cones*, small pyramids of ceramic material which soften and bend when certain temperatures are reached. They were invented by the German ceramist Herman Seger in 1886 and are generally referred to as Seger cones, although there are now other proprietory brands, Orton cones, for example, manufactured. The maturing of clay and the melting of glazes depends on both temperature and time, what potters call heat-work. A slow firing over a longer time causes glazes to melt at a slightly lower temperature than they would otherwise do and vice versa. Cones react to time and temperature in exactly the same way and so are excellent indicators of heat work. They are graded in 20° or 30°C intervals according to the temperature required to soften them and they are very cheap to buy. Cones are placed in the kiln among the pots close to a spy hole where they are clearly visible during the firing. The table shows the numbers and bending temperatures of two widely used cones.

Instruments known as pyrometers are also available for measuring temperature. They work on the principle that when two different metals are fused together and then heated a tiny electric current is generated which is directly related to temperature. A pair of platinum and rhodium wires (the thermocouple) protected by a porcelain sheath is inserted through the wall of the kiln so that it protrudes a little way into the setting chamber. The thermocouple is connected to a dial (the galvanometer) fixed outside the kiln and this indicates the temperature within. Pyrometers only record the temperature where the thermocouple enters the kiln and they are not an accurate indication of heat-work. They are very useful, however, in showing the rise in temperature, particularly at critical stages of the firing process, and for recording the rate of cooling. Pyrometers are fairly expensive and may perhaps be more of a luxury than an essential. To begin with a few cones of different bending temperatures are all that you will really need.

BENDING TEMPERATURES OF PYROMETRIC CONES

Orton Cone	°C	Seger Cone	Orton Cone	°C	Seger Cone
022	600	022		1020	04
021	615		05	1045	03
020	635	021	04	1060	02
	670	020		1080	01
019	685	019	03	1100	1
018	715	018	02	1120	2
	730	017	01	1135	3
017	750	016	1	1150	
016	785	015	2	1165	4
	795	014	3	1170	
015	800		4	1185	5
014	835	013	5	1195	
013	850	012		1200	6
012	885	011	6	1220	
011	895			1230	7
010	905	010	7	1240	
09	925	09	8	1250	8
	940	08	9	1280	9
08	955	07	10	1300	10
07	985	06	11	1320	11
06	1000	05	12	1350	12

NOTE: The bending temperatures above are those given by the manufacturers and based on a rise of 150°C per hour, the rate common in industry. Craft potters will fire their kilns somewhat slower than this and the bending temperature of all cones will, therefore, be lower. To find the lower temperature for any make of cone subtract 25°–30°C from the temperature opposite each cone number, i.e. for cone 8 it will be approximately 1225°C (1250°C minus 25°C).

Chapter 8

Kiln Building

There is a tremendous satisfaction to be gained from firing a kiln built with your own hands. In addition it is possible, with a little planning, to get both more setting space in which to fire your pots for the money spent, and a kiln that meets your specific needs more exactly than one purchased ready-made.

For many potters manufactured electric kilns will be the only ones possible. Circumstances and convenience will always far outweigh their disadvantages. But there are a growing number of others who perhaps began firing with electric kilns and, realising their limitations, increasingly want to explore the more exciting possibilities of other fuels. There is no doubt about it, firing with a living flame is as creative and imaginative an experience as making pots themselves.

It would be unfair to pretend that building a kiln is as easy as buying one, but it really is not as formidable a task as one might think. Far more difficulties exist in the imagination than in practice. There is much to be said for tackling the job as a group project, joining with others in a class or with friends and neighbours who share the pleasures of hand pottery. This divides the cost, helps with the inevitable chores and allows discussion of any queries as they arise. But equally there is no reason why you should not build a kiln alone.

KILN DESIGN
In my experience it is designing a kiln that deters far more than the actual laying of bricks. Many amateurs and even some professionals are daunted by the absence of a specific plan. Some kiln plans are available from oil and gas companies and from some craft organisations, but a plan that shows the position of every brick does not exist. Some plans I have seen are, in fact, more confusing than helpful. A rough ground plan that you can draw yourself showing the main positions of firebox, setting chamber and chimney is really all that is necessary to begin.

Once the first bricks are laid it is astonishing just how clear is the way ahead.

Cost and fear of failure also loom large, and the two are interrelated. Obviously one is wary of spending money on a piece of equipment whose performance is uncertain. But the nature of kilns themselves should offer reassurance on this point. They are *not* precision instruments. The sizes and proportions of fireboxes, flues and chimneys allow for wide tolerances. There is no need to be absolutely specific. So many kiln designs – often quite unlikely ones – work well that it is impossible to describe them all in the space of this or any other book. What I can hope to do is lay down some guide lines you might follow both in the design and the construction of kilns.

The two golden rules of kiln building are:

1. Kilns of simple design and proportion work better than complex ones – and are easier to build.

2. Make all openings through which heat passes (i.e., flues, chimneys etc.) on the generous side so that they can be altered without difficulty. Openings can easily be made smaller; enlarging them is much more difficult.

The information below relates to kilns generally and also specifically to the size of kiln suitable for a keen amateur potter or group. Its capacity is 7 to 12 cu. ft. inside dimensions (24 in deep × 21 in wide × 24 in high to 30 in deep × 24 in wide × 30 in high). This will be space enough to fire 40 or 50 pots at a time, or fewer large ones – which is not too small to limit the size of work nor too big so that firings are infrequent. It would be effective for earthenware or stoneware and offers a choice of oxydising or reducing kiln atmospheres. Gas, oil or wood can be used to fire it.

Some of the kiln design problems will quickly solve themselves. Building or fire regulations will largely determine the kiln site, and the cost of construction and the space available its size. What heats the kiln will be governed by the kind of fuels readily available.

KILN PROPORTIONS

Setting Chamber. The setting chamber should be roughly the shape of a cube if heating is to be even. It can be a little deeper than wide, or higher than wide, but it should not, for efficient working, be wider or deeper than it is high. It is a good idea to base the size on a complete brick length or width. This avoids having to cut too many bricks. An easily divisible brick such as 9 in × 4½ in × 3 in is ideal.

Fireboxes. The size of fireboxes is governed by the kind of fuel. With wood-fired kilns the temperature will not rise high enough unless a sufficient volume of wood is being burnt at any one time. The firebox, therefore, needs to be quite large in relation to the setting space, between one sixth and one quarter of the size, excluding the area below the firebars where the ash collects. The firebars themselves, on which the wood is burnt, will need to be of cast pig-iron to withstand the temperature generated in the firebox.

Fireboxes or combustion chambers for gas and oil can be smaller. For a kiln of 7–12 cu. ft, Rhodes* gives 500 cu. in as the size of combustion chamber for gas burners. From my own experience this seems very generous.

* Kilns: Design, Construction and Operation.

112

Oil burns with a longer flame and requires a combustion area at least twice that of gas. About 1,000 cu. in, the equivalent of a space 9 in × 9 in × 12 in, would be needed for a single oil burner heating a space of 7–12 cu. ft.

The roofs of all fireboxes should be arched, not flat, and the arch should be built right through the wall of the kiln into the setting chamber (for construction of arches see below).

Burners. One large gas or oil burner would heat a kiln of 7–12 cu. ft but two, or even four in the case of gas, would heat more evenly. The number of burners needed depends, of course, on their size and heat output. Burner manufacturers are the best people to consult on this question. They would be able to tell you the heat output of each size of burner they make and consequently the size and number needed to raise any given space to the temperature you want. As a general rule burners should be over rather than under-powered for flexibility when firing the kiln.

Inlet Flues. The space through which the heat passes from the firebox or combustion chamber to the actual setting space, that is the area between the kiln wall and the bag wall, should be three to four times the area of the chimney cross section. If this passage is too small either insufficient heat will pass to the pots or the speed of gases will be too fast and uneven flashing of the glazes may result. If the passage is too large valuable setting space will be lost.

Exit Flues. The spaces through which the gases exit from the setting chamber to the chimney should be at least equal in area to the cross-section of the chimney. If the exit flues are too small they will block the draught and prevent complete combustion taking place in the firebox.

The cross-section area of any horizontal flue joining the setting chamber to the chimney should be approximately that of the exit flues.

Chimneys. For gas and oil a chimney 9 in × 4½ in in cross section will be adequate for a kiln 7–12 cu. ft: For wood 9 in × 6 in would suffice. A convenient rule of thumb is that the height of kiln chimneys should be 3½ times the down-draught. A kiln 30 in high inside will, for instance, need a chimney about 9 ft high.

It is important for the chimney to project above walls or hedges which might obstruct the draught or cause wind eddies.

KILN MATERIALS

The kiln foundations can be of brick or concrete blocks, or a combination of materials such as one would use for any kind of structure, subject to the conditions described below (see Foundations). Construction of the kiln proper will require several kinds of bricks. All must be firebricks of one sort or another, made of materials capable of withstanding the heat and strain of firing.

Where heat is extreme in and around fireboxes or combustion chambers, for load-bearing areas of walls around inlet and exit flues, and for bag walls (see below), high-quality dense firebricks are essential. A kind containing about 60% alumina should be chosen.

The inner hot-face walls of the kiln and the main arch should be of light-weight insulating firebricks. To minimise maintenance these should be capable of withstanding *at least* 100°C (212°F) over and above the maximum temperature of a glaze firing. Thus a kiln firing to cone 10 (1300°C – 2372°F) will need bricks that will not shrink or spall (break up) at 1400°C (2552°F). It is a mistake to build the whole kiln of dense bricks because they absorb heat better used to raise the temperature of the setting space.

For the outer face of the kiln and for chimneys, ordinary wire-cut firebricks (i.e. flat on both sides) or even good quality vitrified engineering bricks are satisfactory and far cheaper than building with insulating bricks alone. My own kiln has wire-cut firebricks on the outside and the only drawback I have found to using them is that the kiln cools rather slowly from about 800°C (1472°F). Common red bricks are insufficiently heat-resisting and should *not* be used. Firebrick manufacturers will supply details of the kinds of bricks available together with their maximum service temperatures. They will also supply fireclay or proprietory refractory cements for bonding and levelling the bricks.

There is no reason why you should not use second-hand refractory bricks for kiln building provided that you are sure they will withstand the temperature or the load you impose on them. But if the vendor cannot tell you for certain their maximum service temperature it could be a costly economy, and on balance I think it better not to take the risk.

KILN CONSTRUCTION

Foundations. These should be obviously solid and capable of supporting the kiln without the slightest risk of subsidence. They may also be built up so that the door is at a convenient height for loading.

When you lay foundations make provision for a damp course. Damp is a kiln's worst enemy because it seriously slows down the heating of the pots. Prevent it from rising into the walls and base of the kiln by placing polythene sheeting or aluminium foil between two layers of concrete. Make sure that the damp-proof membrane is far enough down in the foundations for it not to be damaged by heat.

Ordinary concrete foundations should be at least 4 in thick and protected from heat by an additional layer of refractory concrete, or by two layers of wire-cut firebricks laid end on to make a bed 9 in deep. Lay each layer of firebricks so that the joints do not coincide.

You will find it most convenient to lay down a rectangular foundation block on which firebox, setting chamber and chimney can all be built.

Walls. The minimum thickness of kiln walls is 9 in, comprising an inner $4\frac{1}{2}$ in layer of light-weight insulating bricks and an outer $4\frac{1}{2}$ in layer of ordinary dense firebricks. I think it is easier to build the outer layer first, beginning at the corners and using *only just enough mortar to level the bricks*. I emphasise this point because very firm bonding will cause the brickwork to crack when the kiln is heated. Stagger the joints on each course of bricks.

If the mortar is mixed so soft that it almost flows the job of tapping the bricks into alignment will be much easier. Insulating bricks are very porous, and damping them before spreading mortar will also be a great help. Lay each course of bricks level, straight and plumb, using a line and a spirit level to help you. Careful laying of each course of bricks is worth stressing because corrections are difficult once the walls have got out of line and faults become exaggerated as their height increases. Cut any hard bricks with a hammer and wide masonry chisel: score deeply all round the brick on a line where you wish to cut and then strike sharply along the line with the chisel and hammer. The softer insulating bricks can be very easily cut with a hacksaw and shaped by rubbing. They are, however, very abrasive, so you will need several spare saw blades.

All kilns expand and contract on heating and cooling. If excessive cracking is to be avoided you must, besides using the minimum of mortar, leave an expansion joint $\frac{1}{4}$ in wide between every third or fourth brick, so that the whole structure can 'breathe'. Stagger these joints throughout both inner and outer walls. Occasionally a brick can be laid across both walls to tie them together. Build both walls up to the level from where the arch will spring.

The areas immediately above and around the inlet and exit flues should be of dense, high-alumina bricks. Span the holes for exit flues using a brick as a lintel. With 9 in × 4$\frac{1}{2}$ in × 3 in bricks, lintels 6 in wide are easily made. Inlet flues should be arched because of the greater stress at those points.

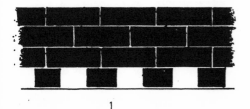

1

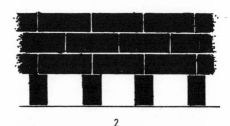

2

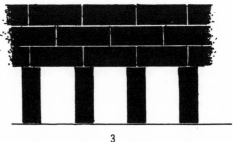

3

57 Different sizes of exit flue using
      standard 9 in × 4$\frac{1}{2}$ in × 3 in firebricks
      as uprights and lintels:
      1 4$\frac{1}{2}$ in square flues;
      2 4$\frac{1}{2}$ in × 6 in flues;
      3 9 in × 6 in flues.

Arches. To aid the flow of gases through the kiln and to distribute the heat evenly kiln roofs are arched. This form of construction sounds formidable, but is actually one of the easiest parts of kiln construction.

Shallow arches are best. They are more stable and prevent cold areas developing at the crown. A rise of 2–2½ in per foot of span is sufficient for most kilns, and 4½ in thickness is all that is necessary. If brick manufacturers are given the dimensions of the kiln and the rise of the arch they will calculate for you the taper and number of bricks needed to build it. Cutting your own bricks to shape is possible, but proper tapering arch bricks are more convenient to use and make a better job.

Although the arch will be self-supporting when completed it must be built over a forma (fig. 58). This is made of wood, using either laths or

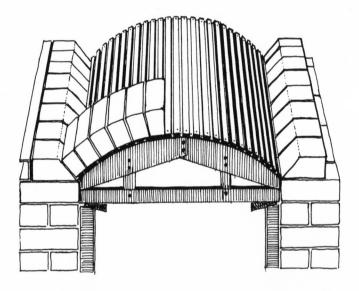

58 Arch forma made from thin strips of wood nailed to a wooden frame

hardboard (Masonite) to join each end. The forma is propped inside the kiln and raised by bricks and wedges until the ends of the arch are level with the top of the walls. The arch is built by first cementing 'skewbacks' to the top of two facing walls. These are wedges of hard firebricks from which the arch will spring. Then the arch bricks themselves are laid in place beginning at each side of the forma and working towards the centre. They should fit close against one another: slight irregularities can be filled with mortar or better still by rubbing two adjacent bricks together to improve the fit. Lastly the centre brick is gently tapped in place, using a piece of wood and a mallet. This last brick is the keystone and a really snug fit is essential. When the arch is complete the wooden forma can be safely removed.

Arched firebox roofs and entry flues for wood-fired kilns are built in exactly the same way using smaller formas. Firebox arches should be two bricks (9 in) deep, the inner arch acting as a forma for the outer one. In this case the outer layer of bricks will have a different taper than the inner ones. The main kiln arch can be constructed only one brick ($4\frac{1}{2}$ in) deep and considerable costs saved by covering it with a further $4\frac{1}{2}$ in layer of insulating material rather than with another course of arch bricks. Vermiculite (expanded mica) is ideal for this. It is usually used for domestic roof insulation, but it will serve equally for kilns. It is non-inflammable, heat-resistant, highly insulating, cheap and readily obtainable from most builders suppliers. It can be poured loose over the arch and contained by building up the outer kiln wall to form a parapet. With my own kiln I mixed refractory concrete with some of it just to bind it across the crown of the arch, from where it might otherwise slip off.

Doors and Spy-holes. There is really no need for hinged doors on any kiln. It is sufficient to leave a space in one wall during construction through which pots can be loaded and unloaded, though this should obviously not be in a wall which is supporting the arch. The door can be quickly filled with firebricks each time the kiln is fired and the gaps sealed with a clay/sand mixture. A door the width of two brick lengths (18 in) is a good size. The edges should be of hard firebrick to withstand the inevitable wear and tear of loading and unloading the kiln, and the bricks laid across both inner and outer layers every other course. If the setting space requires two shelves across its width construct the door to one side instead of in the middle of the kiln wall for easier loading.

Provision should also be made for at least two holes 3 in high by $1\frac{1}{2}$ in wide on each side of the kiln to act as spy-holes. It is through these that you will have your only contact with the pots while the kiln is firing. One hole should be at the top of the kiln just below the crown of the arch and the other level with the lowest shelf on which the pots will stand. Spy-holes can be left in the bricks which block the door and in the back wall of the kiln facing the door. Cut removable bungs from insulating firebricks to plug the spy-holes during firing. A snug taper fit is best, with a good 2 or 3 in protruding from the hole.

Chimneys. Insulating bricks are a luxury for chimneys: ordinary firebricks will be quite adequate. A groove should be left in the chimney during construction for a damper to be inserted. This can be metal (cast iron) but a piece of old kiln shelf is better. It must be capable of closing the chimney completely, and positioned no higher than the crown of the kiln arch. Leave a hole similar to a spy hole in the base of the chimney. You can then pre-heat it with a gas torch or bits of wood on lighting the kiln and get a draught moving through it.

Where the chimney passes close to rafters as it goes through a roof at least 12 in should be left between any wood and the brickwork. Adjacent roof timbers should also be covered with asbestos sheet as an additional precaution against fire. Metal chimneys are an especial fire risk. At this point economies with chimneys can be very costly.

117

Call in professional help to make roofs around chimneys water-tight.

Bag Walls. These are the last part of the kiln to be built. They are walls built of dense firebrick inside the setting chamber at right angles to or parallel with the firebox, depending on the arrangement of the burners. Their purpose is to protect the pots from direct flame impingement. Bag walls about half to two-thirds the height of the setting chamber will generally be sufficient protection for the pots. Build the bricks on their 3 in edge and lay them up dry without mortar so that they can be easily raised or lowered if need be, or so that small gaps can be left between the bricks to allow more heat to pass through the wall into the lower part of the setting chamber.

Bracing. To absorb the thrust of the arch when the structure is hot a piece of steel channel or angle is placed behind the skewback. Angle irons are placed at the corners of the kiln to hold this in place and metal tie rods hold the whole lot together. 2 in × 2 in × $\frac{1}{4}$ in angle and $\frac{1}{2}$ in tie rods are sufficiently strong for small and medium sized kilns. The bracing helps to keep the structure together, although its real purpose is to support the arch. Bracing should never be screwed up too tight, especially when the kiln is cold. If the brickwork cannot 'breathe' it will crack severely.

Arch-roofed fireboxes of wood-fired kilns also need bracing in the same way.

DRYING OUT

All new kilns, even new electric ones, contain a lot of moisture, and it is essential that they are dried out thoroughly before pots are fired in them. Drying out must be very slow and preferably carried out over two or three days with a small flame at one or more of the burners. A butane or propane gas torch is a useful aid for this. When the burners themselves are first lit they should be on their lowest setting for some hours and the kiln then taken very slowly up to a red heat only (1000°C − 1832°F) to allow the new structure to settle gently. Leave a top brick or two out of the door and the bungs out of spy holes.

Kilns mature with age and one ought not to expect too much of the first firing or so. Save your better pots for subsequent ones. Rather use the initial firings to gain an insight into the character of your new kiln, placing various cones throughout to determine the range of temperature. Every kiln is individual and each has its own peculiarities. What these are can only be gained from experience.

Some cracks will inevitably appear in the brickwork despite the expansion joints and careful drying out. This is perfectly normal and no cause for alarm. Small pieces of mortar may also drop from the arch for a few firings, but this will gradually cease as it settles into place. Painting the inside of the

59 (*Opposite*) Elevation and plan of a small down-draught gas-fired kiln

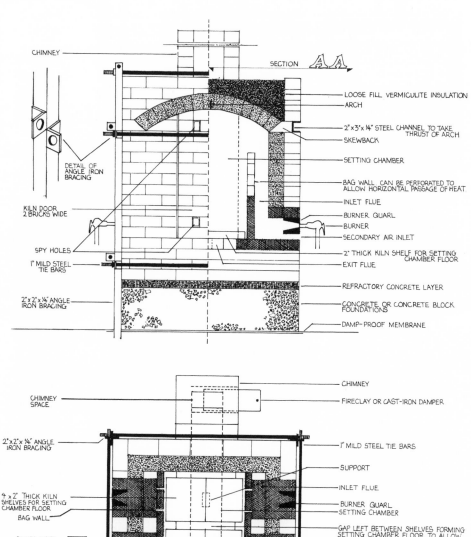

CHIMNEY

SECTION AA

LOOSE FILL VERMICULITE INSULATION

ARCH

2" x 3" x ¼" STEEL CHANNEL TO TAKE THRUST OF ARCH

SKEWBACK

SETTING CHAMBER

BAG WALL CAN BE PERFORATED TO ALLOW HORIZONTAL PASSAGE OF HEAT

DETAIL OF ANGLE IRON BRACING

INLET FLUE

BURNER QUARL

BURNER

SECONDARY AIR INLET

KILN DOOR 2 BRICKS WIDE

2" THICK KILN SHELF FOR SETTING CHAMBER FLOOR

SPY HOLES

EXIT FLUE

1" MILD STEEL TIE BARS

REFRACTORY CONCRETE LAYER

2" x 2" x ¼" ANGLE IRON BRACING

CONCRETE OR CONCRETE BLOCK FOUNDATIONS

DAMP-PROOF MEMBRANE

CHIMNEY

FIRECLAY OR CAST-IRON DAMPER

CHIMNEY SPACE

2" x 2" x ¼" ANGLE IRON BRACING

1" MILD STEEL TIE BARS

SUPPORT

INLET FLUE

4 x 2" THICK KILN SHELVES FOR SETTING CHAMBER FLOOR

BURNER QUARL

SETTING CHAMBER

BAG WALL

GAP LEFT BETWEEN SHELVES FORMING SETTING CHAMBER FLOOR TO ALLOW GASES TO ENTER THE EXIT FLUE

DENSE WIRE-CUT FIREBRICK

HIGH TEMPERATURE LIGHTWEIGHT INSULATING BRICK

DENSE HIGH-ALUMINA BRICKS

SPY HOLE

KILN DOOR 2 BRICKS WIDE

BUNG

SCALE 1:10   0   1   2 FEET.

119

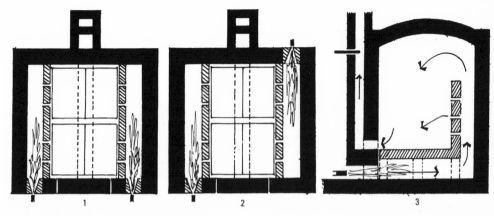

60 Alternative positions for burners
and fireboxes.   1 Two gas or
oil burners firing parallel down
each side of the kiln;   2 Two
gas or oil burners firing parallel
but from opposite corners;
3 Single large gas or oil burner
with firebox under the setting
chamber floor. (All these three
arrangements give good even
heating at both earthenware and
stoneware temperatures);
4 Arrangement of firebox for a
wood-fired kiln. Provision must
be made to allow some heat to
pass under the floor of the setting
chamber to heat the back part of
the kiln.

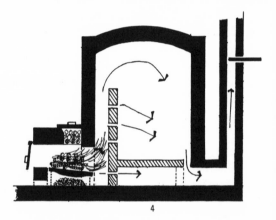

kiln with any spare glaze melting at around 1250°–1280°C (2285°–2336°F)
will help prevent bits flaking off the arch and walls and will also help to
improve heat radiation throughout the kiln.

If your kiln has been constructed according to the second of the two
golden rules mentioned earlier in this chapter, adjustments are easily made
to improve its performance should this prove to be necessary. Flues may be
made smaller by inserting small pieces of brick, bag walls raised or lowered
or openings made in them to allow the horizontal passage of heat, chimneys
made lower or taller, or the paths of heat and flame redirected. This latter
will help to overcome any uneven heating, which is far more likely to occur
than non-heating.

Techniques of firing are not acquired quickly and more kilns fail to perform well because of inexperience on the part of the potter than through
shortcomings in design and construction. The more firings you have the
more your skill and experience will grow. You will come to know something – but never everything – about the peculiarities of your kiln, its faults
and its virtues.

No one can promise that your firings will always be successful, and one must anticipate occasional disappointment. What I can say for certain is that the fire will often fortuitously bestow beauty both on the least significant of your pots and on those which you prize the most.

SAFETY PRECAUTIONS

Kilns are designed to contain intense heat safely and securely and a well constructed kiln should not be a fire hazard, whether it is fired by electricity, gas, oil or wood. Few fires, in fact, originate from kilns themselves. But it is sensible to seek advice from your local fire prevention officer and to take all necessary safety precautions yourself.

1. The most obvious one is that kilns must be soundly built or carefully installed so that there is not the slightest possibility of their collapse during a firing. Never, therefore, economise with materials where safety is concerned, especially in the construction of fireboxes, combustion chambers and load-bearing parts of kilns around the flues. I mentioned above the need for special care where chimneys pass through roofs.

2. Leave plenty of space around and above the kiln so that you can move freely. Keep all clutter off the floor and store combustible materials such as wood, cardboard boxes, cloths, etc. well away from the kiln. Low ceilings and walls very close to kilns are a fire hazard.

3. Fuel-burning kilns, especially during reduction firings, give off carbon dioxide and carbon monoxide gases. These are dangerous only if the kiln room is poorly ventilated. Always ensure, therefore, that plenty of fresh air circulates around the kiln room. Leave doors and windows open, or fit an extractor fan in a wall or roof to draw fresh air into the room.

4. Locate gas and oil storage tanks and wood stacks well away from the kiln.

5. Have a good large fire extinguisher near the kiln where it is easily accessible. Have it regularly checked. Never use water extinguishers on electrical fires.

6. Fit safety pilot lights on gas burners and safety valves on gas and oil supply pipes so that in any emergency fuel can be cut off from all burners simultaneously.

7. When lighting gas and oil burners always place the lighting torch against the burner nozzle *before* turning on the fuel. Light one burner at a time.

8. If burners go out allow plenty of time for raw gases to clear before trying to relight them. In kilns with more than one burner it is safer if one goes out to turn them all out before relighting.

9. Never leave gas- and oil-fired kilns until the area around and in front of the burners is glowing really red hot. Then, if burners go out momentarily they will re-ignite against the incandescent brickwork.

10. Never, in any case, leave any kiln for more than a few minutes. If you have to be absent for a while ask someone to keep an eye on things until you return.

Chapter 9

Glazes

Glazes are coatings of glass which fit over fired clay. They give the clay a smooth surface, impart colour and texture to it and make it more decorative. From a practical point of view they also make domestic pottery more hygienic and easier to clean. In the case of soft earthenwares, glazes make an otherwise porous pottery impervious to liquids.

Glazes differ from glass only in that they have been developed and adapted to the special purpose of covering fired clay. Ordinary glass which is made into bottles or window panes has a low viscosity; when it is melted it is so fluid that it can be moulded, blown or rolled flat. Glazes, in contrast, have a high viscosity; they must be stiff when melted otherwise they would run off the pots instead of adhering to them. Glazes can be smooth, rough, shiny, matt, transparent or opaque, depending on the proportions of the ingredients and the temperatures at which they are fired.

The basis of all glazes is silica, the most common earthly mineral. It is introduced into earthenware glazes mainly in the form of powdered flint or quartz and into stoneware glazes as part of the mineral feldspar. Silica, however, has a very high melting point ($1710°C - 3110°F$) and this is well beyond the temperature that potters' clays can withstand. By itself, therefore silica would be impossible as glaze material. Fluxes must be added to it to lower its melting point.

Particular fluxes determine the temperature at which glazes mature and, to a great extent, also determine their character. The temperature ranges of various glazes are as follows:

700°–900°C (1292°–1652°F)	Very soft earthenwares, including Japanese Raku and many kinds of peasant pottery.
900°–1100°C (1652°–2012°F)	Earthenware, including slipware, majolica and tin-glazed wares.
1220°–1280°C (2228°–2336°F)	Salt-glazed stoneware.
1250°–1320°C (2282°–2408°F)	Stoneware with feldspar-based glazes.
1280°–1350°C (2336°–2462°F)	Porcelain.

Prepared Glazes. Prepared glazes for all temperature ranges are readily available from most potters' suppliers. Some are already coloured. All that

122

is necessary is to mix the glaze with water, cover your pots with it and fire them. Obviously these glazes are both quick and convenient, but you should approach their use with circumspection. They do tend to fall into one of two extremes. Either they are exceptionally bland and characterless, or they are polychromatic eye-strainers with exotic names like Sleepy Lagoon or Spring Fling.

Good suppliers, however, also sell prepared basic glazes to which you can add your own colouring or texturing agents. These are particularly good for beginners. They combine a simple and convenient way of ensuring good and reliable results from the glaze fire with the opportunity for personal experiment and discovery – which, after all, is what any craft is about. The makers clearly indicate the maturing temperature and firing range of these basic glazes and one clear glaze to suit your temperature range will be quite sufficient to begin with.

Mixing Your Own Glazes. Potters' suppliers are also aware that a growing number of discriminating potters increasingly want to formulate and mix their own glazes. As a result they now offer a very wide range of raw materials with which you can do it. Mixing your own is much cheaper than buying prepared glazes, even just basic ones. More important it affords unlimited opportunities for developing glazes which are not only exciting but also highly individual and personal. Mixing your own glazes isn't a difficult job and some glaze recipes which you might like to try are given at the end of this section.

The actual chemistry of glazes is fascinating but highly complex. Most glaze materials are subtle admixtures of several oxides and minerals formed and combined by long, and often little understood, geological processes. Such technical detail is outside the scope of this book, but readers who would like to delve more deeply into the subject are referred to several excellent accounts the titles of which can be found in the appendix.

For the purposes of mixing your own glazes from the raw materials it will be sufficient to look at the two principal kinds of glazes – earthenware and stoneware – and describe briefly the functions of the main ingredients.

EARTHENWARE GLAZES
Earlier in Chapter 7 I described briefly the development of kilns. You will remember that for centuries in both Europe and the Middle East, potters were unable to attain very high temperatures because of the design and construction of their kilns. The maximum temperature in the most efficient of early kilns was probably not more than 1050°C (1922°F) and in many it was much lower. Once glazes were discovered – almost certainly by accident – potters sought by trial and error to find fluxes powerful enough to bring down the melting point of silica to about or just over half, that is to match the temperatures they were able to attain in their kilns. Initially these fluxes were only three in number. They were lead, sodium, and potassium oxides, although obviously they were not available in the pure forms that we can

obtain today. In more recent times boric oxide (borax) has also come into common use as a low-temperature flux. These four fluxes are used singly with silica or in combination with one another, roughly in the proportion of two parts of silica to one of flux.

Unfortunately the above oxides have some serious disadvantages as raw materials for mixing glazes. To begin with lead oxide is highly toxic and its careless use in glaze making can result in lead poisoning. Sodium, potassium and boric oxides are soluble in water and making glazes with other than insoluable materials is very difficult. These two difficulties are overcome, however, by a process known as fritting. This is done by the suppliers of glaze raw materials. They heat the silica and a flux together in a crucible and when the mixture is molten they pour it into a tank of cold water. This cools the mixture almost instantaneously, causing it to fracture into tiny pieces. These are then easily ground into a fine powder which is both non-toxic and insoluble.

Frits, then, are a fired mixture of both silica and flux. They can be used by themselves as a glaze for very low temperatures, but they are generally more satisfactory if mixed with other ingredients to raise their melting point, increase their viscosity, and to make them harder and more durable.

Glazes made with frits as a base vary in their surface quality and in their response to colouring agents according to which particular flux has been fritted with the silica. The particular characteristics of various earthenware fluxes are described below.

Lead Glazes. Lead oxide has been the most widely used flux for centuries and it is still popular today. It is very dependable, and glazes containing it can be relied upon to melt gradually and evenly to produce a smooth shiny surface comparatively free from flaws. Lead glazes also produce rich and brilliant colours with some depth to them. They are particularly satisfying over red clays and were always traditionally used for English slipware, contributing much to its warm and homely character. Lead glazes also have a good relationship with clay and can easily be made to fit it well without crazing. Old potters used to say that lead and clay were made for one another.

Lead glazes are, however, easily scratched unless hard fired. They also have a very low tolerance of reducing atmospheres and unless you have some experience it is safer to fire them in the strictly oxidising atmosphere of electric kilns. Lead oxide very easily reduces to the basic metal, and when this happens the glaze surface boils and discolours. The toxic nature of lead is also a health hazard and in recent years there has been concern over the use of lead-glazed food and storage pots made by hobby and craft potters. Acid fruits and juices served or stored in them can eat into the glaze, freeing the lead from it, and several cases of lead poisoning have resulted from this. Such glazes were almost certainly made with raw and not fritted lead. If fritted lead is used according to the suppliers' instructions the danger of poisoning is negligible. Most suppliers are very mindful of the risks involved in the use of lead glazes. Lead frits, or glazes based on them, bought from reputable merchants have a low lead solubility and comply with safety regulations. If you are in any doubt consult the manufacturer.

Three lead frits based on varying proportions of lead and silica offer a choice of melting temperatures. These are:

LEAD MONOSILICATE – equal parts of lead and silica: temperature range 800°–1050°C (1472°–1922°F).

LEAD BISILICATE – 1 part lead to 2 parts silica: temperature range 900°–1100°C (1652°–2012°F).

LEAD SESQUISILICATE – 2 parts lead to 3 parts silica: temperature range 950°–1100°C (1740°–2012°F).

Of these three lead bisilicate will probably prove to be the most useful for craft potters.

Borax Glazes. The discovery of boric oxide as a powerful low-temperature flux has made possible the development of lead-free glazes. Borax glazes are clear and smooth and fit the clay well. They, therefore, have many of the desirable properties of lead glazes without any of the dangers. Some colouring oxides work particularly well in borax glazes tending towards the brilliance of the alkaline glazes described below. Others, like iron particularly, respond poorly and lack the brilliance they have in lead glazes. One striking feature of borax glazes is their tendency towards a milky opalescence and the addition of small quantities of colouring agents can result in very variegated and interesting glaze surfaces, especially on flat tiles and dishes.

Borax frits are available from suppliers for various temperature ranges between 900°–1180°C (1652°–2156°F).

Alkaline Glazes. These glazes which rely on sodium and potassium oxides as fluxes are perhaps the most exciting of all earthenware glazes. Soda and potash are strongly alkaline, and this fact results in glazes which respond vividly and brilliantly to colouring oxides. The magnificent blues, greens and turquoises of Egyptian, Persian and Hispano-Moresque wares resulted from the use of soda and potash as fluxes in their glazes. All colouring oxides produce stronger and more vibrant colours with alkaline glazes than with any other kind (see colour plate 5).

They have, however, some serious drawbacks. Alkaline glazes, especially low-fired ones, are very soft and easily scratched. Over a period of time they gradually grow dull and deteriorate with even moderate use. They are thus at their best for more decorative wares. They are also rather difficult to fire successfully because potash and soda are such powerful fluxes that earthenware glazes containing them tend to melt suddenly instead of gradually: any over-firing causes them to run excessively. Alkaline glazes are also very difficult to fit well over clay without some crazing. Attempts to cure this by altering the glaze or the clay are seldom successful without either radically altering the character of the glaze or seriously impairing the working properties of the clay. Provided that the pots are only decorative crazing is no real problem, and in fact it can be a distinct decorative feature. Some potters rub stains into the crazing to emphasise it.

Alkaline frits also have a wide firing range, from 750°–1100°C (1380°–2012°F), and glazes fired at the higher temperatures will be the most durable though not necessarily the most colourful.

Other Earthenware Glaze Materials. It will be convenient to mention here several other common materials which are present in many earthenware glazes. We shall come across some of them again in the following section devoted to stoneware glazes, but it will be less confusing to list them here as well, in the order in which quantities are normally given in recipes, because their function at lower temperatures is slightly different.

CHINA CLAY. This introduces both silica and alumina into the mix. Silica raises the melting point of the glaze, while alumina increases viscosity, thereby stiffening the melt and preventing the glaze from running. Being relatively free from iron the introduction of china clay into the mix does not effect the colour of the glaze.

BALL CLAY. Its function is similar to that of china clay. The silica content of ball clay is a little higher, however, and the presence of iron in the clay will add some colour to the glaze.

FELDSPAR. This is a secondary flux for earthenware glazes. It adds silica and alumina to the mix together with small amounts of soda and potash. Its presence increases viscosity in the glaze and also lengthens the firing range.

WHITING (LIMESTONE). Makes the glaze harder and thus more durable. It also renders lead glazes more insoluble and therefore safer to use for domestic pottery.

FLINT OR QUARTZ. This is almost pure silica and additions to the glaze increase its melting point.

TIN OXIDE. Added to the mix in amounts up to 10% it makes a glaze opaque and rather coldly white.

ZINC OXIDE. In quantities between 5% and 15% it produces opacity, mattness and dryness of glaze surface. Too much can lead to glaze flaws developing.

STONEWARE GLAZES

The making of stoneware involves clay in a kind of regeneration. Clay was formed from stone and through the action of the fire it returns to stone. It thus reveals, in a way that earthenware can never do, the earthy and rocky origins of all clays. Stoneware glazes are, in fact, like stones polished and weathered by countless years of geological action. They have such a depth of surface and subtlety of colour and texture that they appeal not only to the eye but also to the touch. It is this tactile quality that makes stoneware so irresistably appealing to many potters.

The basis of all stoneware glazes is feldspar in one form or another. This material is mostly silica with the addition of alumina and a flux, occurring roughly in the proportions of 7 parts silica to 2 parts alumina to 1 part flux. Soda and potash are the two most common fluxes in feldspar, and fortuitously for potters they are present in it in a naturally insoluble form.

You can see, then, that feldspar is a kind of natural frit. All the essential ingredients for a glaze are present in it. It differs in its function from a manufactured lead-silica or borax-silica frit only in that it melts at a higher temperature. Feldspar by itself will melt to a milky-white glaze at about 1250°C (2282°F) but more satisfactory glazes are obtained by adding other materials to it. You will recall from Chapter 1 that feldspar, besides being the basis of all stoneware glazes, is also the matrix of clay itself. As a consequence of this, stoneware glazes have an especially close relationship with fired clay. At higher temperatures the glaze actually becomes part of the clay, and it is impossible to tell where one begins and the other ends. In contrast, earthenware glazes always remain a distinct and separate coating of glass over the fired clay.

Stoneware glazes, like the clay body itself, are extremely tough, hard and durable. They are also non-toxic. While they may lack the strong and even vibrant colours of some earthenwares they compensate by having an endless variety of subtle, quiet colours which reassure as well as excite. Because they contain several fluxes, instead of only one or two, stoneware glazes also melt gradually over a range of 2 or even 3 cones. There is, therefore, little risk of over-firing through quite a wide temperature range.

The following list gives some of the common materials you will come across, together with a brief description of the part they each play in formulating your own stoneware glazes.

FELDSPAR – the basis of all stoneware glazes. They all contain between 40% and 70%. It occurs naturally in various kinds which differ slightly from one another. These are:

1. Potash (Orthoclase) Feldspar. This has more potash than soda as the flux. It is the one generally used where a glaze recipe calls simply for feldspar.

2. Soda (Albite) Feldspar. This has more soda than potash. It melts at a slightly lower temperature than 1 above.

3. Nepheline Syenite. A feldspar with an unusually high proportion of soda and potash in relation to the silica content. As a result its melting point is less than 1 and 2 above, and it may be used where it is necessary to slightly lower the melting point of a glaze.

CORNISH STONE (CHINA STONE). A kind of feldspar found in Cornwall, England, where the soda and potash are in about equal amounts. It is also higher in silica, with the result that it melts at slightly higher temperatures than other feldspars.

QUARTZ OR FLINT. This adds pure silica to the glaze. It increases its melting point, makes a glaze shinier and helps glaze fit by inhibiting crazing.

CHINA CLAY AND BALL CLAY. Clay adds silica and alumina to the glaze roughly in the proportions of 2:1. It stiffens the glaze melt and prevents it running and also imparts hardness and durability. Depending on the quantity it can also increase or lessen the degree of glaze shine. Clay also toughens the raw glaze coating before firing and makes handling the pots much safer.

WHITING (LIMESTONE). This is a strong flux in small quantities, though in too large amounts it tends to have the opposite effect making a glaze matt and opaque.

TALC (MAGNESIUM SILICATE: FRENCH CHALK). This adds silica and magnesia to the glaze and also acts as a secondary flux. It imparts opacity and depth to some glazes.

DOLOMITE. This contributes magnesia and calcium to the glaze in roughly equal parts. It makes glazes more matt and gives them a particularly attractive satin or sugary surface.

BONE ASH (CALCIUM PHOSPHATE). Small amounts cause opacity and opalescence in the glaze. It also imparts a lovely soft sheen to the surface of some glazes.

WOOD ASH. This is not charcoal but the fine mineral powder remaining after the complete combustion of wood. Its presence in the glaze can yield particularly soft colours or variegated surfaces which are very appealing. Wood ash is an unpredictable material, but is often valued by stoneware potters for that very reason. It contributes silica, alumina and flux in the form of soda or potash, but in exactly what proportions it is impossible to say because of the enormous number of variables involved. The chemical composition of wood ashes varies according to the kind of wood it is, the sort of soil in which it grew, even according to the season of the year. The ash of oak, elm, ash, apple, pine and reeds are all suitable for glazes. If you

128

burn the wood yourself do it slowly, or a lot of charcoal will be left; otherwise gather it from wherever you can. You will need what seems to be quite a lot to begin with because the usable quantity left after washing and sieving will only be a small proportion of the amount gathered.

To prepare the ash place it in a large bucket and cover it with water. Any charcoal still in it will float to the surface and can easily be skimmed off. Sieve the mixture – first through a garden sieve to remove any coarse particles, and then through an 80-mesh. Discard any material retained by the sieve. Allow the ash to settle in the water for a day or so and then decant the water from the top. Wash the ash to remove the soluble alkalies by adding more water, stirring vigorously and again leaving to settle. Do this again until the water becomes fairly clear. Two or three changes of water will probably be sufficient. After the final decanting dry the ash thoroughly. It will then be in a fine powder form and ready to use.

Use wood ash as a basis to formulate glazes of your own. Very simple glazes of great beauty and variety can be made using only wood ash, clay and felspar as ingredients.

HOW GLAZES MELT

At the start of a glaze firing each pot is coated by a powder made up of all the raw glaze materials finely mixed together. This powder coating remains inert until the interior of the kiln begins to glow red. At this stage carbon and sulphur present in the glaze materials start to volatilise and are driven off. As the heat advances to a bright red the glazes begin to 'sinter', that is to form a hard tough coating as some of the materials begin to melt. This sintered glaze coating may be very rough and under a microscope would resemble crocodile skin. With greater heat more of the glaze ingredients are drawn into the melt and as this happens the process of melting accelerates. The glazes become increasingly liquid and may pass through a stage where they resemble boiling water. The surface becomes disrupted and cratered as gases pass through the glaze and burst. With more heat and time these eruptions gradually cease and at the top temperature the glazes settle over the pots and assume a smooth clear surface.

When the kiln is shut off and the glazes begin to cool they gradually harden until they solidify at about 600°C (1112°F). Between 270° and 200°C (548° and 392°F) the clay body shrinks a little, thereby slightly compressing the glazes. This is the ideal state for glazes, as mild compression ensures that they fit the pots well without crazing.

COLOUR IN GLAZES

Glazes are coloured by the oxides and salts of various metals. They are added to the glaze mix in fine powder form and are gradually pulled into the melt, forming crystals within the glaze. The amount of colouring oxide or combination of oxides should, wherever possible, not exceed 10% of the total mix. The particular glaze colour and its intensity are largely determined by the kind and quantity of oxide used. The most common oxides and some of the colours they produce are described below. It may appear strange that some oxides give such a wide range of colours but this is because glaze colour is not entirely the result of the oxide alone. Other factors also play a part. Among these are the colour of the underlying clay body, the nature of certain glaze materials themselves, the thickness of the glaze relative to the clay, the maturing temperature of the glaze, and the prevailing kiln atmosphere – whether oxidising or reducing. A white or coloured slip will also affect, and itself be affected by, the colour of the glaze over it.

With such a list of variables the colours resulting from metal oxides are unlimited in number. Much of the pleasure and excitement of glazes comes from discovering what colour each oxide will produce with your own particular clay and firing conditions.

Iron Oxide. Iron oxide is by far the most important and versatile colouring agent. Added to glazes in amounts from 1–10% it produces an extraordinary range of colours. For earthenware iron is at its most brilliant in low-fired glazes containing a high proportion of lead. Small amounts (1–4%) produce lovely rich amber and honey colours while larger amounts (5–10%) give shades ranging from rich chestnut and mahogany browns to deep blue-black. Iron is more subdued in alkaline glazes. In glazes containing tin oxide as an opacifier the addition of iron yields interesting mottled and variegated creams and browns, depending on the quantity used.

For stoneware glazes iron is at its best in glazes fired in reduction. Amounts of 1–2% produce the glazes known as celadons, pale greeny-grey or grey-blue glazes which at their best have the deep opalescence of jade. Shades of olive green result from 3% of iron, while 4–6% produces green-brown glazes. The range of saturated iron glazes known as 'hare's fur' or 'tenmoku' contain 8–10% of iron. These handsome glazes with a rich and varied brown-black streaked surface break to a characteristic rust-red where the glaze runs thin on rims and edges of handles. Oxidised stoneware glazes containing iron give colours ranging from pale amber through dark brown to brown-black, but they often lack the lively surfaces of reduced wares. In amounts above 7% some oxidised iron glazes tend to develop an unpleasant metallic appearance.

Red iron is the oxide most commonly used in glazes, but there are other iron oxides, all of which produce slight variations on the above range of colours. Among these are yellow ochre, which is a weak colouring oxide, and black iron oxide, which is coarser than red and which produces a more blue-grey rather than green-grey colour in celdaons. Magnetic iron spangles and crocus martis, crude iron oxides, both give speckled effects in glazes. Iron chromate, a mixture of iron and chrome, produces a range of subdued grey-browns.

Oxides, especially iron, act as fluxes in glazes, lowering their maturing temperature and their viscosity. The presence of even small amounts will make a glaze noticeably more fluid, and larger amounts can result in an over-fired glaze running down and off a pot. On cooling the glaze seals the pot firmly to the kiln shelf, from where only a cold chisel will remove it. A wise precaution is to leave a good ¼ in of unglazed foot on any pots covered with a glaze containing a high percentage of oxide to allow for any slight running.

Copper Oxide. Copper produces blues and greens and is principally used in earthenware glazes. It is added to the glaze mix either as finely ground light green copper carbonate or as coarser black copper oxide. Both copper oxide and carbonate are powerful colourants and they should be used sparingly. The addition of 1% to a glaze will produce light greens, 2–3% gives strong greens, while 3–5% results in broken, matt, greeny blacks. Amounts in excess of 5% almost invariably make the glaze black and the surface unpleasantly metallic.

In lead glazes copper gives soft warm shades of grass and leaf green. In highly alkaline glazes, especially those containing very little alumina, 1–2% produces the vibrant blue-greens of some Egyptian and Persian pottery. The colour intensity of this kind of copper blue glaze is improved by the choice of a pale clay or the use of a white slip under the glaze.

For stoneware copper is rather unreliable as a colouring agent. It becomes volatile at temperatures about 1250°C (2282°F) sometimes affecting the colour of other glazes in the kiln as it escapes from the glaze as a vapour. In heavily reducing atmospheres copper may give a variety of reds as the oxide reduces to the basic metal. The famous Sang-de-boeuf glazes of the old Chinese potters were achieved in this way. But the atmospheric kiln conditions necessary for achieving copper red glazes are very critical and some measure of good luck is essential for repeated success.

Cobalt Oxide. Cobalt gives various shades of blue. It is a very stable and reliable colourant for all temperature ranges, being unaffected by either high temperatures or reducing atmospheres. It is also extremely powerful and very tiny amounts will produce strong colours. One quarter of 1% added to a glaze will give a distinct blue, while 1% will produce a very dark blue. The use of more than 1% will give blue-black or black.

Nearly all blues resulting from the addition of cobalt alone are harsh, insistent and uniform in surface. Consequently most potters choose to modify the colours by adding small amounts of other oxides such as iron, manganese, nickel or chrome. Very subtle and beautiful blues, blue-greens and blue-greys can be obtained in this way. When cobalt is added to glazes with a high magnesia content very lovely and interesting purple and lilac colours often result.

Cobalt is used either in the form of cobalt carbonate or black cobalt oxide. Of the two the carbonate is usually preferred, as it is more finely ground and a less powerful colourant.

Manganese Dioxide. Manganese gives purples and browns. Compared with some oxides it is a weak colouring agent and 2–4% must be added to

131

produce a discernible colour. It will give a rich blue-purple in alkaline earthenware glazes, but in most other kinds it tends towards a rather dull brown. It is probably of greater use in modifying other more powerful oxides than as a colourant in its own right. Add manganese to the glaze either as finely ground manganese carbonate or as coarser manganese dioxide. Small amounts of the latter kneaded into clay bodies will produce interesting spots and speckles.

Chromium Oxide. In lead glazes fired below 950°C (1742°F) yellows, oranges and reds may be obtained by the addition of 1–2% of chromium oxide. Small quantities (one quarter to half of 1%) added to earthenware glazes containing tin oxide as an opacifier will produce shades of warm browny pink. Small quantities of chrome, about 1% or less, will subtly modify the blues produced by cobalt in reduced stoneware glazes.

Nickel Oxide. Small amounts of nickel oxide will produce greys or grey-browns but the use of more than $1\frac{1}{2}$–2% results in dull and dingy browns. Nickel is a useful oxide for modifying copper and cobalt colours.

Vanadium Pentoxide. This is supplied by potters' merchants usually in the form of vanadium stain, a mixture of vanadium pentoxide and tin oxide. The addition of 5% to a glaze will produce a weak yellow while a strong yellow will require up to 10%.

Tin Oxide. Tin oxide is added to transparent glazes to make them white and opaque. Its use is confined mainly to earthenware but it can be added to stoneware glazes, when the resulting white is rather stark and cold, especially in reduction firings. Small amounts of tin oxide (1–3%) will make a glaze semi-opaque white; larger amounts from 5–10% make a glaze densely white and fully opaque. Semi-opaque tin glazes are very attractive over red clays because of the way they subtly reveal the warmth of the clay body.

COLOURING AGENTS IN OXYDISED GLAZES

% Added	Agent	Fired Colour
$\frac{1}{2}$–3	Chrome Oxide	Orange, yellow, red, green. Pink (with tin oxide).
$\frac{1}{4}$–1	Cobalt Carbonate Cobalt Oxide	Pale to dark blue.
1–4	Copper Carbonate Copper Oxide	Grass green to green-black.
1–10	Iron Oxide	Pale amber to dark brown-black.

% Added	Agent	Fired Colour
4–8	Manganese Carbonate Manganese Dioxide }	Pale to darker purple-brown.
$\frac{1}{2}$–2	Nickel Oxide	Grey to brown.
2–10	Tin Oxide	Semi-opaque to dense opaque white.
5–10	Vanadium Stain	Pale to strong yellow.

COLOURING AGENTS IN REDUCTION GLAZES

% Added	Agent	Fire Colour
1	Chrome Oxide	Variegated blue-green (with $\frac{1}{2}$% Cobalt).
$\frac{1}{4}$–1	Cobalt Carbonate Cobalt Oxide }	Pale to dark blue.
$\frac{1}{2}$–3	Copper Carbonate Copper Oxide }	Dark pink red to red-black (unpredictable).
1–2$\frac{1}{2}$	Iron Oxide	Celadon glazes – pale grey-greens to dark olive greens.
4–5	Iron Oxide	Variegated green-browns.
8–12	Iron Oxide	Dark red-brown to rich black 'tenmoku' glazes.
4–6	Manganese Carbonate Manganese Dioxide }	Light to darker browns.
$\frac{1}{2}$–2	Nickel Oxide	Grey to brown.
2–5	Tin Oxide	Cold opaque white.

FORMULATING GLAZE RECIPES

Although I mentioned earlier in this section that the actual chemistry of glazes is highly complex there is no reason why this fact should prevent any keen potter from conducting meaningful experiments in order to formulate simple glaze recipes of his or her own. By doing so you will certainly gain greater satisfaction from making hand pottery and, equally important, come to a greater knowledge and insight into the nature of clay and glaze materials. Potters, like other craftsmen, can never have enough knowledge of the materials they use.

All principal glaze ingredients are oxides of one kind or another. Some, like clay and feldspar, are subtle and intimate combinations of several oxides. Consequently it is important to realise that when adding certain glaze materials to a mix you are, in effect, putting in not just one but two, three or even more substances simultaneously. There is a very accurate scientific method of determining exactly how much of any one oxide is present in a given glaze by calculating the weight of the molecules in each oxide. Readers who have an elementary knowledge of chemistry and the patience for arithmetic should find this method well within their capabilities. It is clearly described in several of the reference books listed in the appendix. But equally good glazes can be formulated by a more practical trial-and-error approach. Indeed all the finest glazes of the past, many of which surpass in beauty any we do today, were arrived at in this empirical way.

On pages 126 and 127–8 I described briefly the function of various common glaze ingredients, and by using that basic information it should not be difficult to work out a few simple glaze recipes of your own.

The most important thing is that glazes should melt to a smooth glassy coating over your pots at a given temperature. It is the principal flux in each glaze which largely controls its melting temperature and which almost invariably constitutes the main glaze ingredient. The simplest and easiest approach to formulating your own glaze recipes is, therefore, to decide the approximate temperature at which you want your glazes to melt and then choose the appropriate flux for that temperature range. For earthenware the flux will be lead, or borax, or soda and potash, usually in a safe, insoluble fritted form. For stoneware the main ingredient will be one of the feldspars, potash feldspar itself, Cornish stone or nepheline syenite.

Suppose, for example, you wished to formulate an earthenware glaze. You could begin by taking a lead frit such as lead bisilicate as your starting point. By itself lead bisilicate will melt to a glaze at about 900°C (1652°F) but it would melt rather suddenly, be too fluid and have too soft a surface to be a satisfactory and durable glaze. The addition of some alumina would help to stiffen the melt, while some silica would make the glaze harder. At the expense of the lead bisilicate, a small amount of china clay, which is mostly alumina and silica, would add the ingredients necessary to form a more satisfactory glaze. This would give a simple recipe of:

Lead Bisilicate   90 parts   China Clay   10 parts.

If more refractory materials are added at the expense of the flux the melting temperature and hardness of the glaze will increase. A series of simple glazes which melt at increasingly higher temperatures might look like this:

| TEMPERATURE RANGE °C (°F) | | INGREDIENTS – PARTS BY DRY WEIGHT | | |
		Lead Bisilicate	China Clay	Flint
A	900–1000 (1652–1832)	90	10	—
B	1000–1050 (1832–1922)	80	10	10
C	1050–1100 (1922–2012)	70	15	15

Some flint is added to glazes B and C because the alumina content of china clay will, if used in excess, dull the surface of the glaze. The addition of flint which is almost pure silica will help to keep the glaze clear and bright while also raising its melting point.

Borax or, if strong and vibrant colours with copper and cobalt are wanted, alkaline frits, could be used as a starting point. If the glaze does not melt sufficiently add a little more flux at the expense of the more refractory ingredients, and vice versa if the glaze is too fluid. Once the glaze is melting properly at the temperature you want then add other ingredients to make it opaque or give it colour or texture or all three.

Unlike earthenware glazes, which can be made to melt below 900°C (1652°F) to just over 1100°C (2012°F), stoneware glazes melt in a very narrow temperature range between 1250°C (2282°F) and 1320°C (2408°F). This is partly because high-temperature fluxes are comparatively less powerful than low-temperature ones, and also because the melting temperature of stoneware glazes are closely tied to the vitrification temperatures of the clays they cover. Feldspar is the only material potters have which will melt within the temperature range and, in consequence, all stoneware glazes contain between 40% and 70% of it.

An average, therefore, of 50–55% of feldspar is a good starting point for experimenting with stoneware glazes. Feldspar will craze over nearly all clay bodies because of the quantity of soda and potash it contains. The melt would also tend to be a little too fluid. Some silica in the form of flint would help the glaze to fit, and some alumina in the form of china clay would stiffen the melt. Both these materials are very refractory and some additional flux such as whiting may also be necessary. Bearing these factors in mind we might arrive at a simple satisfactory glaze recipe consisting of:

| Feldspar | 55 | China Clay | 20 |
| Whiting | 15 | Flint | 10 |

This will melt to a slightly milky opalescent glaze at cones 8 to 9 (1250°–1280°C – 2282°–2336°F).

Most stoneware glazes are satisfactory over a range of 2 or even 3 cones (20°–60°C to 68°–140°F). Consequently, changing the proportions of some of the glaze ingredients, particularly the silica and alumina, often alters the character of the glaze surface more than it raises or lowers the maturing temperature. You can prove this for yourself by rearranging the proportions of the china clay and flint content of the above glazes and testing the different recipes given in the following table.

| GLAZE | INGREDIENTS – PARTS BY DRY WEIGHT | | | |
	Feldspar	*Whiting*	*China Clay*	*Flint*
A	55	15	25	0
B	55	15	20	5
C	55	15	15	10

| GLAZE | INGREDIENTS – PARTS BY DRY WEIGHT | | | |
	Feldspar	*Whiting*	*China Clay*	*Flint*
D	55	15	10	15
E	55	15	5	20
F	55	15	0	25

Glazes C, B and A, in that order, will be progressively more opaque, duller and drier in surface while glazes D, E and F, in that order, will be progressively shinier and clearer.

One of the advantages of higher temperatures is that often some quite surprising materials will melt to form glazes. Pebbles from the beach or rocks from the hillside or quarry will, if crushed to a fine powder, sometimes sinter or melt to form a glaze at stoneware temperatures. Some domestic scouring powders are actually made from ground feldspathic rock and will form a crude glaze. Interesting, exciting and personal glazes can be made by mixing these kinds of local found materials with feldspar. Various wood ashes, too, can yield particularly beautiful glazes with a wide variety of subtle colours and textures. A basis for experiments might be as follows:

| | PARTS BY DRY WEIGHT | | | | | | | | | | |
	A	*B*	*C*	*D*	*E*	*F*	*G*	*H*	*I*	*J*	*K*
Wood ash, crushed local stones, pebbles etc.	100	90	80	70	60	50	40	30	20	10	0
Feldspar	0	10	20	30	40	50	60	70	80	90	0

Testing new glazes can be very wasteful of materials if you are only able to measure comparatively large amounts. The ingredients of glazes are usually given in percentages and even using a unit of weight as small as an ounce will mean 100 oz of dry glaze materials as a minimum amount. When mixed with water this quantity will give about half a bucketful of glaze. A pair of scales, therefore, with $\frac{1}{4}$ oz divisions or, better still, a chemical balance with gram divisions, is an invaluable help in weighing small quantities of glaze for experiments and tests.

It is, in any case, unwise to mix up a large quantity of untried glaze and cover many pots with it. If the glaze is not very appealing you are left with unattractive pots and if the results are disastrous – if the glaze runs badly for instance – you could lose not only the pots but valuable kiln shelves as well.

It is better and safer to try new glazes first on very small pots thrown from off the top of a cone of clay. These are quickly and simply made and can be left unturned. Or you can use test rings of clay which take up a negligible amount of kiln space. Such rings are easily made by looping a thin coil of clay round your index finger and pinching off any surplus just beyond the overlap. By pressing the ring onto a board with your finger on the overlap the join will be flattened out to form a stand for the ring. As the ring dries it will shrink away from the board. Tiny pots have one advantage over rings in that they show the effect of glazes on a vertical surface. Both pots and rings should, of course, be biscuit-fired before being used.

When experimenting with glazes the importance of weighing materials accurately and of keeping careful and accurate records of recipes, firing schedules, kiln temperatures and atmospheres cannot be too highly stressed if much valuable work is not to be lost. Each glaze test should be marked indelibly on the base of the ring or pot, using iron or cobalt oxide mixed with a little water. The code number or letter used should correspond with a particular glaze recipe. Only in this way will you know which recipe produces which glaze. More frustrating than the failed glaze test is the outstandingly successful one of unknown recipe!

Don't abandon the apparent failures too readily. Surprisingly rich and lovely glazes can result from covering one seemingly uninteresting glaze with another of similar kind. I keep a tub of a white glaze which by itself is undistinguished but which, when put over a brown iron glaze gives a particularly rich and handsome black tenmoku glaze.

SOME GLAZE RECIPES FOR YOU TO TRY

Below are the recipes of some dozen of so glazes which I have found to be generally reliable and which might form a basis for further personal experiment. They cover the whole range of temperatures from low-fired soft earthenware to high-fired stoneware and porcelain. The ingredients of the glazes will, however, almost certainly vary according to their origin and from supplier to supplier. Firing schedules and conditions will also vary from potter to potter. The advice given above about careful testing applies, therefore, to them as to any other new glazes.

GLAZE RECIPES

Maturing Cone	Ingredients	Parts by Dry Weight	Description
08	Lead sesquisilicate	74	A low-temperature lead frit
	Feldspar	16	glaze. Clear when thin,
	China Clay	4	more opaque when applied
	Whiting	3	thickly.
	Flint	3	

Maturing Cone	Ingredients	Parts by Dry Weight	Description
05	Alkaline Frit Flint China Clay Copper Oxide Cobalt Oxide	84 8 4 2·5 1	A brilliant blue-green alkaline glaze with a rather soft surface. It will craze over most clay bodies.
04	Lead bisilicate Feldspar Whiting China Clay Flint	61 25 6 4 4	A clear, bright glaze. Good over slip decoration or with added oxides.
03–01	Borax Frit Feldspar China Clay Tin Oxide	74 15 11 5	A semi-opaque white leadless glaze.
01	Lead Bisilicate Feldspar China Clay Whiting Tin Oxide	56·5 31 7 5·5 10	A dense opaque white glaze. Good over red clays.
01	Lead Bisilicate Cornish Stone Ball Clay Bentonite	71 13 12 4	A lead frit glaze suitable as a raw clay glaze.
8	Feldspar Flint China Clay Whiting Talc Red Iron Oxide	30 26 11·5 14 5·5 10	A dark brown to black glaze which breaks to lighter colour on rims and handles. It has a smooth, bright surface but tends to run if over-fired.
8–9	Feldspar China Clay Whiting Flint	48 22 20 10	A milky opalescent glaze with semi-matt surface Good for added oxides.

Maturing Cone	Ingredients	Parts by Dry Weight	Description
8–10	Wood Ash Feldspar China Clay	50 25 25	A matt glaze with richly varied surface. Its colour depends upon the kind of ash used. For best results apply by pouring.
9–10	Feldspar Wood Ash Ball Clay	40 40 20	A semi-matt glaze particularly good in reduction. Colour depends on the kind of ash and ball-clay used.
9–10	Cornish Stone or Feldspar Flint Whiting China Clay Talc Zinc Oxide	 37 22 22 13 4·5 1·5	A smooth bright glaze good for added oxides, especially iron.
9–11	Feldspar Ball Clay Talc Red Iron Oxide Flint Whiting	60 18 15 10 5 2	A smooth semi-matt iron glaze. Under a celadon it will produce a 'tenmoku' glaze if fired in reduction.
10–12	Feldspar Flint Whiting Talc China Clay Zinc Oxide	37 36 17 4·5 4·5 1	A smooth, bright pale glaze for high-fired stoneware and porcelain. Apply thinly on porcelain for best results.

Chapter 10

Glazing and Glaze Firing

GLAZING

Preparing Biscuit Ware for Glazing. Biscuit-fired pots intended for glazing must be dry and free from dust or grease. Brush off any particles of sand or grog used for setting the pots in the biscuit kiln.

Paint with hot wax those parts you wish left unglazed. These will probably include foot rings, the undersides of lids and flanges, and inside the galleries of lids. Great economies of kiln space are possible by firing lids in place, but it is essential that the rims are completely free from glaze otherwise the lid and pot will fuse together in the firing. As an additional precaution against sticking lids, especially at higher temperatures where the risk is greatest, paint a creamy mixture of sieved china clay and water under the wax.

Now is also the time to do any brush decoration, using either colouring oxide mixed with water and a little gum arabic or a half glaze – half oxide mixture. The former mixture will give sharp bold effects, the latter more subtle ones. In both cases the colour intensity of the brushwork will depend upon the thickness of the paint mixture.

Glaze Mixing. Mix glazes carefully and methodically. Apart from the colouring oxides all glaze ingredients are very similar white powders, so before you begin make sure that all the raw material containers are clearly marked. The failure of glazes to perform as expected can often be the result of wrong labelling, returning surplus ingredients to the wrong container or, most often, to just forgetting to add the whole or part of one of the ingredients. It is a wise precaution to list the ingredients and tick them off one by one as you add them to the mix.

Weigh all the ingredients carefully, crush up any large lumps with a rolling pin, and place them in a bucket or tub. About ten pounds of dry materials will fill a two gallon bucket with finished glaze. Add water, and leave the mix to stand for a while until the water has had time to soften any smaller lumps. Then stir the contents thoroughly with your hand, adding more water if necessary, until the liquid is the consistency of thick cream. Don't have the mixture too thin at this stage or you will have to wait for a day or so while the glaze ingredients settle before you can decant surplus water.

Pass the mixture through a 120-mesh sieve into a second container using

a stiff brush (fig. 61). A mesh this fine is delicate, so be careful not to scrub too hard or you will damage it. Add a cupful of water to the mixture in the sieve if, from time to time, the mesh becomes clogged. Make sure that no unsieved glaze enters the second container without passing through the mesh, and also that as much of the ingredients as possible goes through to preserve the correct proportions of the recipe. Some materials, particularly dolomite and wood ash, are stubborn in this respect. If glazes containing a high percentage of clay and wood ash are still lumpy after sieving pass them through an 80-mesh first and then through a 120-mesh. Glazes of this kind also tend to settle very readily into a stiff mass at the bottom of the bucket. The addition of half a cupful of vinegar will help to prevent this.

When sieving is completed cover the glazes unless you intend using them immediately. Above all, label each one very clearly: like the ingredients, many sieved glazes look the same.

Glaze Application.   Decide which glazes you are going to put on particular pots and assemble them in groups so they can be dipped in batches successively in each glaze. You will need a separate jug and stick for pouring and stirring each glaze, plus a bowl of water and small sponge for wiping off any surplus or drips.

Only experience will teach you the correct consistency for a glaze. Generally

141

speaking it should be rather creamy, but the thickness of the glaze coating will also depend on the thickness and porosity of the biscuit ware and on the length of time the pot is immersed in the glaze. You can adjust the consistency by decanting surplus water off the top or by adding more. Many glazes will give quite different results depending on their thickness. Where one glaze is applied over another both should be a little thinner than if each were used alone.

It is important that the glaze is well stirred before you begin dipping and that *it is kept well stirred*. The ingredients imperceptibly settle to the bottom, leaving on the surface a thin film of water which can wash most of the glaze off the pot as you withdraw it from the mix. It is very difficult to see that this has happened until it is too late, after the pot has been fired.

Glaze the inside of a pot as follows: fill the pot with glaze using a jug and then quickly pour it out, revolving the pot as you do so to ensure the whole area is covered. Immediately it is empty give the pot a violent shake and a twist of the wrist to remove any surplus and to disperse the glaze coating evenly over the surface. Wipe off any drips on the outside with a damp sponge (fig. 62).

Glaze the outside by one of several methods most appropriate to the size and kind of pot. For earthenware pots with glazed bottoms grip the pot by expanding a hand inside it and then plunge it right way up until the glaze is level with the rim. Shake and twist it to remove any surplus and then

62   Glazing inside

63 (*Above*) Hand hold
   for glazing outside

64 (*Right*) Plunging a
   pot in the glaze

place it on a board as soon as the glaze has dried. This will only be a matter of moments because of the porosity of biscuit ware. Touch up any unglazed parts of the rim with a brush.

For stoneware pots with unglazed bottoms hold the pot with your thumb on the base and your middle finger on the rim (fig. 63). Plunge it upside down into the glaze stopping short of the base (fig. 64). Withdraw the pot, shake and twist it, then turn it over and slide it onto a board. Before you remove your hand just kiss the rim lightly with the tip of a wet finger to touch up the unglazed part where you gripped the pot.

With large pots use both hands, placing one on the rim the other on the base. The outsides of pots too large for dipping can be glazed by pouring. Support the inverted pot on two triangular-sectioned sticks over a container (this method was more fully described on page 88).

The inside and outside of very small pots can be glazed all in one double-dipping action. Grip the pot between thumb and finger and invert it. Plunge it into the glaze up to the base, jerk it quickly out and plunge it in again swiftly. This sharp movement creates an upward splash of glaze which covers the inside.

Grip flat pieces such as dishes, plates and tiles with a finger or hand on either edge of the rim. Do not plunge them in vertically but move them through the glaze in an arc to prevent air bubbles being trapped. A pair of metal tongs with fine gripping points is a useful tool for glazing this kind of flat shape as it absolves you from having to touch up any finger marks (figs. 65 and 66).

Glaze tea and coffee pots as follows. First fill the inside with glaze, then pour just sufficient – and no more – out through the spout to ensure glazing the inside of that. Quickly invert the pot and pour the remainder out through the top. If all the glaze is poured out through the spout it absorbs so much water, being thin, that very little glaze will adhere to the outside of it. After emptying the pot blow down the spout to clear any blockage of the strainer holes. As soon as the glaze has dried plug the end of the spout with a piece of stiff clay and glaze the outside by any of the methods described above (fig. 67). Remove the clay plug and touch up any blemish with a brush or wet finger.

When glazing learn to dip pots quickly and confidently, so that there is no hestiation in the movements. Biscuit ware is so absorbent that there is

65   Glazing a lid by gripping the flange. The rim and flange have been painted with wax to prevent the glaze adhering to them.

66 Dipping a flat dish using a pair of tongs

67 Plugging the spout of a teapot before glazing the outside

145

no need to hold it in the glaze for any length of time. However, if you do make a mistake, wash the glaze off the pot, dry it thoroughly, and try again. Where wax has been incorporated in the glazing use very hot water to ensure that all of it is removed.

Decorating Glazed Pots. Apart from brushwork under the glaze many of the techniques used for slip decoration may be employed to decorate pots after they have been dipped. Glazes can be combed to reveal the clay beneath, although this must be done very swiftly immediately after dipping before the glaze coating becomes soft and powdery. Sgraffito may be done in exactly the same way. Patterns can be trailed or poured over the surface using contrasting glazes. Paper- and wax-resist decoration can be used straight on the biscuited body or between two layers of glaze. Two glazes used in this way should have roughly the same melting point, otherwise any pattern may be blurred or even lost.

Contrasting glazes may also be applied to the raw glazed surface by brush. This is the glaze-on-glaze technique used for decorating majolica and faience. The pot is first dipped in a white opaque glaze which remains stiff when melted and the pattern is painted with coloured glazes on this background. The contrasting glazes are made up of the background glaze plus added oxides. Generally the thinner you have the glaze the higher the concentration of oxide needed. When the pots are fired the decoration melts into the background glaze to form a pattern with soft, diffused edges.

It can be rather frustrating trying to paint on a powdery raw glazed surface, and majolica decoration should, therefore, be done as soon as possible after dipping, before the glaze gets too dry. If you have difficulty you may find it helpful to spray a thin solution of gum arabic over the surface to make a less powdery background on which to paint.

Wiping Off. Before you load the pots in the kiln inspect each one. With a damp sponge wipe off any patches or spots of glaze which may inadvertently have got on the unglazed bottoms of pots or between lids and galleries. Rub a finger over the powdery glaze surface and smooth down any unintentional drips of glaze.

GLAZE FIRING
The glaze firing is the exciting climax, the culmination of all your work. It cannot be too highly stressed that preparing for and managing the fire demands as much, if not more, sound craftsmanship as any other part of the making process. Pots are offered to the kiln more for blessing than for sacrifice, and the inevitable risks of firing, especially at higher temperatures, can be minimised by paying close and careful attention to detail. There will be occasional losses and disappointments, but I am sure that more good work is lost in the kiln through ignorance, carelessness, and more especially through complacency, than through any apparent fortuitous malevolence on the part of the fire itself.

146

Setting the Glaze Kiln.   Arrange your pots in similar sized groups close to the kiln so that it is easy to select pieces for a certain height of shelf. You will be able to pack the kiln more tightly if you have a variety of sizes and rather more pots than the kiln will hold. If the kiln fires unevenly – and many have a variation of a cone or even two from top to bottom – it is also convenient to have glazes which mature at different temperatures to accommodate any uneven heating.

Begin packing at the back of the kiln and move forward as the stacks of shelves are filled. Handle the pots carefully, and touch up any bare or chipped patches if necessary. Place three props, two on adjacent corners and one in the middle of the opposite side of the bottom shelf, and then set the pots between them. They can be packed tightly, within a quarter of an inch of one another, but they must not actually touch. Earthenware pots glazed on the underside must be raised up from the shelf on spurs or stilts: the unglazed bases of stoneware and porcelain pots should be fully supported on flat and level shelves otherwise they will warp as the clay softens during vitrification. Fill in any gaps with smaller pots if you can; air is a poor conductor of heat and the more pots that occupy the available space the better the exchange of heat between them.

Once the bottom shelf is filled carefully cover the pots by lowering another shelf onto the props. Place successive props directly on top of the ones below, so that all the weight is on the floor of the kiln and not on individual shelves. Always select shelves of adequate thickness to support the weight of pots standing on them.

Sieve a thin coating of powdered flint or quartz onto the top of each shelf to prevent pots from sticking. Brush the undersides carefully to remove any dust or foreign matter which might fall onto the pots below and become embedded in the melting glaze.

Put cones on shelves where they can be clearly seen through the spy holes. You will need three successively numbered cones at each point; one to warn you of the approaching maturing temperature, one to indicate that you have reached it and one to show that you have not over-fired the kiln by exceeding it. Set the cones at an angle of about ten degrees in a wad of very well-grogged clay one behind the other. Make sure they can bend and fall without touching either one another or the side of any pot.

If your spy holes are wide enough to allow them passage it will be a great additional help to glaze a few biscuit-fired test rings and place them in front of the cones. At the height of the fire the rings can be hooked out with a long wire to see that the glazes have completely melted.

Pots can be safely set on the top shelf to within half an inch of the arch. If you can, save some of your taller pieces for the top of the kiln. Finally, close the door and clear away all clutter from around the kiln. Leave the sealing of brick doors until the firing is under way.

Glaze Firing (Oxydised).   Glaze firings in electric kilns will automatically be oxydising at all temperature ranges because no fuel is actually being burnt. All you need do is switch on the kiln elements and gradually raise the temperature by following the procedure below until the cones bend.

With other types of kiln it is essential that sufficient air enters the firebox or combustion chamber at all times to ensure complete burning of the fuel. If gas and oil burners are set at the correct air-to-fuel ratio on lighting up, the flame will be oxydising throughout the firing, provided that this ratio is maintained as the burners are turned up to gradually increase the heat. With wood-fired kilns there will inevitably be some smoke, but predominantly oxydising conditions will prevail provided that there is a good pull of air through the kiln and wood is added a little and often rather than in large quantities intermittently.

You can easily tell whether the kiln is oxydising or not by looking through the spy-holes once the inside is glowing red hot. The atmosphere should appear clear and the outline of the pots sharply defined with no flames licking round them. In addition there should be a pull of air into the kiln at the bottom spy-hole. If these conditions prevail and the temperature does not rise it is usually a sign that too much air is being drawn in. This both cools the flame and pulls the heat out of the kiln by convection.

Biscuit-fired pots have a greater resistance to heat shock than raw ones, and from cold the temperature of the glaze fire may be increased fairly rapidly at about 100°C (212°F) per hour to within 100°C of the maturing cone. Then the rate must be slowed right down to allow any volatiles to escape through the glazes and for the latter to gradually smooth over. This process does take time, and a rise in temperature of about 30°C to 50°C (85°F to 120°F) per hour would not be too slow. Aim to allow a half to a whole hour between the bending of the first two cones. When the second one has fallen and the end is touching the shelf try to maintain the maximum heat for about an hour by turning down the heat slightly. This 'soaking period', as it is called, during which the top temperature remains constant, will greatly improve the quality of the glazes. It is a great temptation to rush this period and great restraint is called for if you want to get the best results.

If you have test rings in the fire now is the time to hook them out with a long wire at about twenty-minute intervals. The colour and texture of the glaze on the ring will not be the same as on the pots because the rings cool so very rapidly, but they will give you an excellent indication as to whether or not the glazes have properly melted.

Once you are satisfied that this has happened turn off the kiln or let the fire burn through, as the case may be, seal the kiln and leave it to cool.

Glaze Firing (Reduced). Reduction firings have become increasingly popular because of the greater subtlety of colour and variety of glaze surface which they produce. They are confined almost exclusively to stoneware and porcelain, because low temperature glazes, especially lead-based ones, have a poor tolerance of reducing atmospheres.

An oxydising atmosphere is maintained in the kiln from lighting up until

68 (*Above*) Using a long wire to hook a red-hot draw trial ring through a spy hole

69 (*Right*) The author's kiln being loaded for stoneware glaze firing. The pyrometric cones and draw trial rings can be seen mid-right by the tubular shelf prop.

the glazes begin to sinter between 1000°C (1832°F) and 1100°C (2012°F). Any reduction before this temperature may deposit carbon in the open pores of the clay, causing it to swell and bloat, or the glazes to be pitted and pin-holed. It is quite a good idea to soak the kiln in a strongly oxidising atmosphere at around 1000°C (1832°F) just before reduction starts by letting in an excess of air. This may cause the temperature rise to falter, but it will help to burn off any carbon in the clay. Begin reducing at around 1000°C (1832°F) or 1050°C (1920°F).

With gas and oil-fired kilns this is done by cutting back both the primary and secondary air supplies slightly and, at the same time, pushing in the damper to create back pressure in the kiln. You can check that reduction is taking place by removing the bungs from the spy-holes. A short tongue of yellow flame should lick out of the holes, the atmosphere inside the kiln should appear slightly cloudy and the outline of the pots diffused. If no flame appears push the damper in a little more or increase the supply of gas or oil slightly or both until it does so.

With wood-fired kilns the supply of secondary air should be cut back and the damper pushed in to create back pressure in the chamber. Maintaining a constantly reducing atmosphere is extremely difficult with wood and in practice the atmosphere will alternate between strongly reducing and slightly oxidising: each new baiting with wood will produce reduction followed by a short period of oxidisation as the fire dies back a little and combustion becomes complete. The best one can do is to maintain a *predominantly* reducing fire.

Judging the degree of reduction is very largely a matter of experience with any kind of kiln, but if you pay particular attention to three or four crucial points reduction should be adequate and even throughout the kiln.

1. The damper must be pushed in far enough to create slight back-pressure at the lowest level of the setting chamber, so that a tongue of flame exits from the bottom spy-hole when the bung is removed. Maximum pressure is always at the crown of the arch and it decreases progressively downwards. If there is very little or no pressure at the bottom of the kiln reduction there will be poor, or may not take place at all.

2. It is important also to realise that with advancing heat the speed of gases through the kiln slowly increases, and this leads to a gradual return to oxidising conditions. From time to time, therefore, the damper may need to be pushed in a little more to maintain the same degree of reduction.

3. A small amount of flame at the damper or an occasional light whisp of smoke from the chimney are also signs that reduction has passed right through the lowest settings of the kiln.

4. When reduction is too heavy the temperature in the kiln remains static and may actually fall because of the quantity of unburnt fuel passing through the kiln. Smoke, as well as flame, at the spy-holes, constant black smoke at the chimney and a strong sulphurous smell are all signs of excessive reduction. The damper should be opened a little or the fuel supply decreased

slightly, or both. Very heavy reduction merely wastes fuel, causes unnecessary pollution and can harm both the clay and the glazes.

The rate of temperature increase during the reduction period should be between 30°C (85°F) and 50°C (120°F) per hour. Reduction itself will tend to slow the rate down because of incomplete combustion. With a little experience you should be able to strike a balance between adequate reduction and a gentle temperature rise by adjusting the fire and the damper. Continue reduction until about 1230°C (2245°F) or 1250°C (2280°F), and then return to an oxydising fire for the last 30°C (85°F) or 50°C (120°F). You must do this gradually by pulling out the damper and opening the secondary air supply little by little and, if necessary, adjusting the fuel supply so that there is no sudden increase of heat over the period when the cones begin to bend (fig. 70).

Take a half to a whole hour between the bending of each cone and soak at the maximum temperature for a further hour. This will allow the glazes

70 Melted cones. The guard cone is still upright.

to mature and the heat to spread evenly through the kiln by radiation. Re-oxydisation of the surface of any unglazed clay gives it a lovely warm colour and imparts a brilliance to iron glazes and brushwork. If you draw test rings out of the kiln break one in half to see that the iron oxide in the clay is reduced to grey iron all the way through. Finally, when you are satisfied that the glazes are fully matured, turn the kiln off and allow it to cool.

Keep a careful record of each glaze firing, noting particularly times and temperatures; burner, air, and damper settings; when reduction, if any, began and ended; and the quality of the resulting pots. Record also the weather, as this can have a considerable effect on the draught through the kiln. Over several firings a picture will emerge of your kiln's characteristics and peculiarities and of a firing schedule which you can follow with a reasonable certainty of success.

Cooling the Glaze Kiln. Once the glaze firing is over turn off the fuel or allow the fire to burn down and then seal the kiln tightly. Block the fireboxes or combustion chambers, completely close the damper and clam up all cracks with a sand/clay mixture to prevent cold draughts from striking the cooling pots. Leave the kiln to cool slowly to about 100°C (212°F), at which temperature it can safely be opened.

You can cool high-temperature stoneware kilns very rapidly from their maximum heat to 1000°C (1832°F) and then seal them tightly at that temperature. At the end of the firing open all air inlets and pull out the damper to allow air to sweep through the kiln. The temperature will fall very quickly to 1000°C (1832°F) in the space of about two hours. This in no way harms the pots (the danger from cold air is below 1000°C); in fact, it nearly always improves the quality of the glazes, especially ones containing iron, by preventing crystallisation. It also helps to eliminate body-glaze tensions.

FAULTS AND FLAWS
From time to time some of your pots may develop faults and flaws in the glaze firings. The ones you are most likely to meet, their causes and their remedies are listed below.

1. *Underfiring*
CAUSE: The process of melting was not complete when the kiln was switched off and the pots have a rough and harsh surface as a result. Some earthenware glazes may be smooth but filled with tiny bubbles.

REMEDY: Refire the pots to a slightly higher temperature or hold the maximum heat for a longer soaking period, or both.

2. *Overfiring*
CAUSE: The firing has exceeded the maturing temperature of the glazes. Overfiring is indicated by glazes running off vertical surfaces and pooling around the base of the pots; matt glazes becoming shiny and perhaps also crazed; or by blurred decoration. Severe overfiring may cause glaze surfaces to bubble and blister, or the clay to seriously warp and deform.

REMEDY: Over-fired pots are lost. All one can do is to profit from the mistake and fire to a lower temperature next time using lower cones. Keeping a firing record so that you can refer to burner settings and maximum temperatures is an invaluable help in solving this kind of problem.

3. *Crazing*
CAUSE: This may be because of over-firing, but the appearance of tiny cracks all over the surface is nearly always the result of the glaze contracting more than the clay during cooling. Crazing may take place in the kiln or shortly after the pots are taken from it. The familiar pinging sound of pots newly taken from the kiln is an indication that crazing is taking place.

REMEDY: A small addition of silica to the glaze mix in the form of powdered flint or quartz will generally prevent this trouble. With certain glazes some

71 Overfiring: the glaze has run down both pots, and on the right has become so fluid that some has run off the pot and adhered to the refractory dot on which the pot was fired.

72 A severe case of over-firing in an electric kiln. The object on the left was made from red (terra cotta) clay, as on the right, but this clay has turned to slag; the inch thick refractory shelf has warped and split; and the shelf prop in the foreground has begun to melt.

153

crazing will be inevitable without radically altering their characters. High alkaline soda and potash earthenware glazes, and stoneware glazes containing a high proportion of china clay fall into this category.

4. *Shivering and Peeling*

CAUSE: This is the reverse of crazing. On cooling the clay has contracted more than the glaze leaving it in a state of great compression. In its mild form the glaze peels off the rims or the edges of handles; at its most severe it can cause the pot to burst especially if the pot is thin and the glaze thick, or if the pot is glazed on the inside only.

REMEDY: Decrease the silica (flint or quartz) content of the glaze mix or increase the proportion of feldspar.

5. *Cracking*

CAUSE: The reasons for pots cracking are many. They may be:

(a) Biscuit firing faults which were unnoticed during glazing and which only come to light after the glaze firing. Fine cracks round the base of pots, cracks where handles etc. join are of this type. They are always permeated by glaze.

(b) Cracks caused by too rapid cooling, uneven cooling or cold air striking the pots at a critical stage (dunting). This kind of crack usually runs in from the rim and has no glaze between its split edges.

(c) Spiral cracks running up and through the pot wall. These may be present either when the pots are taken from the kiln, or they may develop suddenly shortly afterwards. Spiral cracks are nearly always the result of too high a percentage of silica in the clay body.

REMEDY: In the case of:

(a) See biscuit faults, page 97.

(b) Seal the kiln more effectively.

(c) Reduce the silica content of the clay by adding to the body 10% to 15% of china clay or similar amounts of a ball clay containing about 30% alumina.

6. *Pitting and Pinholing*

CAUSE: When glazes come from the kiln covered in tiny pits and pinholes it is nearly always because volatile matter has not had sufficient time to escape nor has the glaze had time to smooth over. Heavy reduction may have deposited carbon in the pores of the clay. During the oxidising period at the end of the firing the carbon forms carbon monoxide gas which passes through the glaze disrupting the surface.

REMEDY: Raise the temperature more slowly at the end of the firing; soak at the maximum heat for a longer period; reduce less heavily; or any combination of the three.

7. *Crawling*

CAUSE: Pots come from the kiln with bare patches where the glaze has

73 Pitting and pin-
holing caused by
over-reduction.
Carbon trapped in
the glaze has
erupted violently
through the glaze
surface.

rolled away from the clay. It may be caused by excessive shrinkage of the raw glaze coating before it melts; or because the glaze is too thick; or, and most likely, because dust or grease on the biscuit ware prevent the glaze coating from adhering closely to it.

REMEDY: Rub your finger lightly over any cracks on the raw glaze surface; glaze more thinly; or make sure that biscuit ware is clean and dry, wiping it over with a damp sponge if necessary.

8. *Bloating*

CAUSE: When fired clay is swollen and blistered in places it may be the result of air pockets in the clay, but more often than not it is a fault of the firing conditions. It is mostly confined to high-temperature firings, and is a result of carbon being trapped in the clay by vitrification.

REMEDY: Wedge and knead the clay more thoroughly; or, if it is a result of firing conditions, maintain a strictly oxydising atmosphere to 1000°C (1832°F) and reduce less heavily, particularly in the early stages of reduction.

9. *Uneven Heating*

CAUSE: This is the result of either:

(a) Too fast a firing which does not allow time for the heat to spread through the kiln by radiation, or

(b) faulty kiln setting. Pots and shelves have been arranged in such a way that the draught has been obstructed in certain places.

REMEDY: Allow plenty of time for soaking the kiln at the maximum heat; set the pots so that the heat is more evenly distributed.

10. *Uneven Reduction*

CAUSE: This may take one of two distinct forms. Either some parts of the kiln are reduced and others not, or individual pots are reduced on one side

155

but not on the other. Where the first has occurred it is because of insufficient back-pressure throughout the whole setting chamber. The second phenomenon is because of too lively a draught: the reduction gases have whipped through the kiln, taking very distinct paths between the pots.

REMEDY: The answer in both cases is the same, to create more back-pressure and slow down the draught through the kiln by closing the damper a little more.

11. *Kiln Mishaps*

CAUSE: Some accidents to pots in the glaze kiln are the result of what one can only call bad luck and about these one can do nothing. But most of the others – shelves bending and breaking, props splitting, glazes running, lids sealing, pots stuck together, foreign bodies embedded in the glaze, cones bending and touching pots – are mainly caused by carelessness or complacency.

REMEDY: Take every care in setting and firing the kiln.

74 The author and part of his workshop

Appendix

BASIC EQUIPMENT FOR A SMALL POTTERY WORKSHOP

Raw Materials

2 cwt red (terra cotta) clay.

2 cwt white or buff clay.

1 cwt of fine grog or sand for mixing with clay and for setting pots in the biscuit firing.

1 cwt of plaster of Paris for making clay drying slabs and dish moulds.

½ cwt of basic transparent glaze to which you can add colouring oxides or opacifiers.

½ cwt of ground flint or quartz for modifying glazes and for dusting kiln shelves for the glaze firing.

Equipment

A stout table or wedging bench.

A small kiln, preferably not less than 2 cu. ft internal dimensions, fired by whichever fuel is most suitable for your requirements and circumstances.

Sufficient shelves and props to fill the kiln, plus a few spares.

A selection of cones for both biscuit and glaze firing temperature control.

A pyrometer is also a useful addition if you can afford it.

A good rigid kick or power wheel plus a selection of turning tools and throwing batts – essential only if you want to make pots by throwing.

Several ware boards about 30 in long by 6 or 9 in wide by ½ in thick for drying and carrying pots.

2 large plastic tubs or bins with well-fitting lids for storing clay.

Several buckets with lids for sieving and storing slips and glazes.

Some large sheets of lightweight polythene (polyethylene) in which to wrap damp pots.

A length of hessian or burlap.

3 phosphor-bronze sieves:

　　One 30- or 40-mesh for sieving grog, sand, wood ash etc.

　　One 80-mesh for sieving slips.

　　One 120-mesh for sieving glazes.

A soft brush for rubbing clay and glaze materials through the sieves.

A large artificial sponge for general cleaning.

A pair of scales for weighing clay and glaze materials.

Tools

Plenty of twisted wire for wedging and throwing.

A clay trimmer.

A selection of modelling tools made of boxwood, bamboo or wire.

2 small natural sponges.

A rolling pin and rolling guides.

2 kidney-shaped scrapers, one rubber, the other metal.

A pair of calipers.

Brushes for decorating green or biscuit ware.

For Further Reading

BOOKS

A Potter's Book by Bernard Leach. Faber, London and Transatlantic, New York. Many editions since 1940.

Clay and Glazes for the Potter by Daniel Rhodes. Pitman, London and Chilton Co., Philadelphia, 1957.

Kilns: Design, Construction and Operation by Daniel Rhodes, Chilton Co., Philadelphia, 1968.

Pioneer Pottery by Michael Cardew. Longman, London, 1969.

Pottery: the Technique of Throwing by John Colbeck. Batsford, London and Watson-Guptill, New York, 1969.

Simple Pottery by Kenneth Drake. Studio Vista, London and Watson-Guptill, New York, 1966.

Stoneware and Porcelain by Daniel Rhodes. Chilton Co., Philadelphia, 1959.

The Appreciation of the Arts 6: Ceramics by Philip Rawson. Oxford University Press, London and New York, 1971.

The Technique of Pottery by Dora Billington. Batsford, London, 1962.

Understanding Pottery Glazes by David Green. Faber, London, 1963.

MAGAZINES AND JOURNALS
The leading ceramic periodicals listed below publish technical and general articles of interest to craft potters and also illustrate many aspects of contemporary ceramics. Some contain classified advertisements for second-hand pottery equipment.

Australia
Pottery in Australia, 30 Turramurra Avenue, Turramurra, New South Wales.

Canada
Tactile, Canadian Guild of Potters, 100 Avenue Road, Toronto.

New Zealand
New Zealand Potter, P.O. Box 12 – 162 Wellington North.

FOR FURTHER READING

U.K.

Ceramic Review, the journal of the Craftsmen Potters Association of Great Britain, William Blake House, Marshall Street, London, W.1.

Pottery Quarterly, Northfields Studio, Northfields, Tring, Hertfordshire.

U.S.A.

Ceramics Monthly, Box 4548, Columbus, Ohio 43212.

Craft Horizons, the journal of the American Crafts Council, 44 West 53rd Street, New York, N.Y. 10019.

Studio Potter, Box 172, Warner New Hampshire.

Index

List of U.S.A. Suppliers

Pottery materials, equipment and tools of all kinds

AMERICAN ART CLAY CO. INC.	4717 West 16th Street, Indianapolis, Indiana 46222.
STANDARD CERAMIC SUPPLY CO.	P.O. Box 4435, Pittsburg, Pa. 15205.
STEWART CLAY CO. INC.	133 Mulberry Street, New York, N.Y. 10013.
WESTWOOD CERAMIC SUPPLY CO.	14400 Lomitas Avenue, City of Industry, California 91744.

Clays

CANNON AND CO.	Box 802, Sacramento, California 95804.
CEDAR HEIGHTS CLAY CO.	50 Portsmouth Road, Oak Hill, Ohio 45656.
DENVER FIRECLAY CO.	2401 E. 40th Avenue, P.O. Box 5507, Denver, Colorado 80217.
LANGLEY CERAMIC SERVICE	413 S. 24th Street, Philadelphia, Pa. 19146.
TRINITY CERAMIC SUPPLY CO.	9016 Diplomacy Row, Dallas, Texas.
UNITED CLAY MINES CORPORATION	101 Oakland Street, Trenton, New Jersey 08606.

Electric Kilns

A. D. ALPINE	353 Coral Circle, E. Segundo, California 90245 (also gas kilns).
AMERICAN ART CLAY CO.	4717 W. 16th Street, Indianapolis, Ind. 46222.
L AND L MANUFACTURING CO.	Box 348, Twin Oaks, Pa. 19104.
PARAGON INDUSTRIES INC.	Box 10133, Dallas, Texas 75207.

SKUTT AND SONS	2618 S. E. Steele Street, Portland, Oregon 97202.
UNIQUE KILNS OF TRENTON INC.	530 Spruce Street, Trenton, New Jersey 08638 (also gas kilns).

Gas Burner Equipment

DFC CORPORATION	P.O. Box 5507, Denver, Colorado 80217.
FLYNN BURNER CORPORATION	425 Fifth Avenue, New Rochelle, N.Y. 10802.
JOHNSON GAS APPLIANCE CO.	Cedar Rapids, Iowa 52405.

Gas Kilns

ALLIED ENGINEERING CORPORATION	4150 E. 56th Street, Cleveland, Ohio 44105.
WEST COAST KILN CO.	635 Vineland Avenue, La Puente, California 91746.

Kiln Shelves and Props

KANTHAL CORPORATION INC.	Bethel, Connecticut.
EDWARD ORTON JR. CERAMIC FOUNDATION	1445 Summit Street, Columbus, Ohio 43201.
STEWART CLAY CO.	133 Mulberry Street, New York, N.Y. 10013.
S. PAUL WARD INC.	601 Mission Street, P.O. Box 336, South Pasadena, Clifornia 91030.

Oil Burner Equipment

HAUCK MANUFACTURING CO.	P.O. Box 26, Westchester, Illinois 60153.

Oil Kilns

DENVER FIRECLAY CO.	2401 E. 40th Avenue, P.O. Box 5507, Denver, Colorado 80217.

Refractory Bricks, Cements etc.

B AND B REFRACTORIES CORPORATION	1192 Rivira Road, Santa Fe Springs, California 90670.
A. P. GREEN FIREBRICK CO.	Mexico, Mo. 65265.

JOHNS-MANVILLE CO.	22 E. 40th Street, New York, N.Y. 10016.
NEW CASTLE REFRACTORIES	101 Ferry Street, St. Louis, Mo. 63147.

Wheels

A. D. ALPINE INC.	353 Coral Circle, El Segundo, California 90245.
H. B. KLOPFENSTEIN AND SONS	Route 2, Crestline, Ohio 44827.
RANDALL POTTERY INC.	Box 744, Alfred, N.Y. 14802.
PAUL SOLDNER	Box 918, Aspen, Colorado.
DENTON VARS	825 West Minnehaha Avenue, St. Paul, Minn. 55104 (Leach kick wheel).

For additional information about potters' suppliers apply to :

THE RESEARCH AND EDUCATION DEPARTMENT,
AMERICAN CRAFTS COUNCIL,
44 West 53rd Street, New York, N.Y. 10019.